Praise for The PLC Book

The PLC Book *is a must-read for anyone wishing to establish a PLC in their school, from the leader looking for a whole-school approach, to the classroom practitioner seeking to connect with a group of educators.*

—Liane Pitcher-Leigh
Evidence-Based Teaching Lead, Dene Magna School
Gloucestershire, United Kingdom

The PLC Book *is as essential as* The Reflective Educator's Guide to Professional Learning Communities! *Their careful guidance and realistic examples support the work of teachers to genuinely learn together based on inquiry, shared common goals and reflective practices.*

—Donnan Stoicovy
Elementary Principal/Lead Learner, Park Forest Elementary School
State College, PA

The PLC Book *creates a powerful and memorable connection between the idea of professional learning communities and the actuality of creating and sustaining them.*

—Teri Schrader
The School Reform Initiative, Watkinson School
Hartford, CT

The PLC Book *will be a go-to resource for teachers, from those looking to begin PLCs for the first time to experienced PLCs looking to refine their collaborative work and get more focused on what makes a difference for student learning.*

—Jennie Beltramini
K–8 Math Instructional Coach, Anacortes School District
Anacortes, WA

Dana and Yendol-Hoppey have blazed a path of professional development that few have been brave enough to tackle. They understand schools and how they operate on a core level.

—Jodi Bergland Holen
Professor, University of North Dakota
Grand Forks, ND

As no one else, Nancy Dana and Diane Yendol-Hoppey master the art of bringing innovative theories into the practice.

—Rik Vanderhauwaert
Director, DNI
Belgium

For Gene

The PLC Book

Nancy Fichtman Dana

Diane Yendol-Hoppey

CORWIN
A SAGE Company

FOR INFORMATION:

Corwin

A SAGE Company

2455 Teller Road

Thousand Oaks, California 91320

(800) 233-9936

www.corwin.com

SAGE Publications Ltd.

1 Oliver's Yard

55 City Road

London EC1Y 1SP

United Kingdom

SAGE Publications India Pvt. Ltd.

B 1/I 1 Mohan Cooperative Industrial Area

Mathura Road, New Delhi 110 044

India

SAGE Publications Asia-Pacific Pte. Ltd.

3 Church Street

#10-04 Samsung Hub

Singapore 049483

Acquisitions Editor: Dan Alpert

Associate Editor: Kimberly Greenberg

Production Editor: Amy Schroller

Copy Editor: Megan Markanich

Typesetter: C&M Digitals (P) Ltd.

Proofreader: Dennis W. Webb

Indexer: Judy Hunt

Cover Designer: Anupama Krishnan

Marketing Manager: Maura Sullivan

Printed in the United States of America

Library of Congress Cataloging-in-Publication Data

Dana, Nancy Fichtman, 1964-

The PLC book / Nancy Fichtman Dana, Diane Yendol-Hoppey.

pages cm

Includes bibliographical references and index.

ISBN 978-1-4833-8265-4 (pbk. : alk. paper)

1. Professional learning communities. I. Yendol-Hoppey, Diane. II. Title. III. Title: Professional learning communities book.

LB1731.D34 2015

370.71'1—dc23   2015029284

This book is printed on acid-free paper.

15 16 17 18 19 10 9 8 7 6 5 4 3 2 1

Contents

List of Figures

Foreword

Recently I received a phone call to remind me to renew my theater subscription for the upcoming year. Subscription prices increase each year and recently have escalated substantially, causing me to weigh more thoughtfully my decision to renew. When my hesitation was evident to the salesperson, she asked why I had continued my subscription membership for so long. I found myself thinking aloud about the reasons I subscribed. I not only enjoyed the intellectual stimulation that theater provided but I also enjoyed the experience of being a part of live performance. It transported me into different lives and places instantly. Watching plays unfold enveloped me in magic of the story and acting and the mystery of the technical aspects. A night at the theater usually meant dinner and a night away from the routine of daily life. It provided both entertainment and education simultaneously.

On the top of my list for continuing to subscribe was the theater's commitment not only to provide extraordinary theater experiences but also to investing in the future of theater by commissioning playwrights, presenting readings of new plays, and producing original plays—all with remarkable success. Nurturing the theatrical arts requires ongoing creation of new works and developing playwrights, actors, and the vast array of technical staff.

The PLC Book is an investment in the continuous improvement of collaborative learning in schools. Just as the theater I described previously invests in the continuous development of theatrical products and people working in the field on and behind the stage, so too does a purchase of this book become an investment in a powerful form of collaborative professional learning that research confirms improves both teaching practice and student learning. A recent study by Matthew Ronfeldt, Susanna Owens Farmer, Kiel McQueen, and Jason Grissom (2015) is one of many that confirms that the quality of teacher collaboration matters in increasing student achievement in math and reading. The study suggests that teachers improve more rapidly in schools with better quality collaboration as well.

Dana and Yendol-Hoppey describe the kind of instructionally focused collaboration that improves teaching and student learning. In this book, they weave together scholarly and practitioner voices to cultivate readers' understanding about professional learning communities (PLCs), explain why they are powerful forms of professional learning, depict what they look like in action, and delineate how to initiate or refine existing ones. What makes *this* PLC book different from others are its clarity, simplicity, specificity, and conversational tone. The authors believe that the PLC structure and process must be easy to navigate if it is to be used by teachers to address the complex problems they face in their daily work. If implementation of the PLC is overly complicated, teachers' effort and focus will be distracted from the real purpose of PLCs and their natural inclination to inquire, learn, apply, analyze, and reflect.

The book builds on the best of Dana and Yendol-Hoppey's past work to present new information that includes the essential elements of healthy PLCs and the core cycle of learning teams use to answer their research questions. Building on the criteria of effective PLCs advanced by Learning Forward's (2011) standards and the definition of professional learning (Killion & Roy, 2009), they recommend different approaches to structuring PLCs for different types of teams. They map out the process for orchestrating learning among team members, designing action learning plans, using protocols appropriate for each phase, and designing action learning plans that engage educators in professional learning that leads to changes in instruction and student learning. They emphasize the importance of using data to inform learning and sharing learning within and across teams.

Dana and Yendol-Hoppey offer detailed examples in the forms of reader's theater, narrative, and metaphor to illuminate the PLC process. They introduce the value of protocols that serve as guides and share descriptions of many of them. They invite readers to interact with the text by offering several learning tasks PLCs can use to promote their own learning about PLCs and their PLC success.

Reading *The PLC Book* is both entertaining and educative. It is easy to enjoy the book and to use it again and again as a reference for initiating or fine-tuning PLCs so that they focus on the kind of collaboration about teaching and student learning that intellectually challenge teachers, tap into their professional expertise, stretch their learning, and strengthen their practice. This kind of collaboration undoubtedly will lead to greater success for all students.

—*Joellen Killion*

Acknowledgments

We are grateful to the many outstanding educators we have had the honor and privilege to engage with throughout our careers in learning community work and other forms of job-embedded learning. We have learned a tremendous amount with and from so many dedicated teachers and administrators. While they are too numerous to name individually in this text, we thank you all for opening up your professional and personal lives to us in the intimate work of job-embedded professional learning and in the quest to make schools better places for all.

Our families continue to wrap our writing projects in their love and support. Thanks to Tom, David, Greg, Kirsten, Caran, Billy, and Kevin. We also thank our editor at Corwin, Dan Alpert, for his vision to reinvent material from many of our previous works to create *The PLC Book* and his help and support throughout the writing process. Thanks also to Kimberly Greenberg and Cesar Reyes at Corwin!

Our conceptualization of learning community work has been greatly influenced by Gene Thompson-Grove, who, in both her current efforts leading the School Reform Initiative (SRI) and past work with the Annenberg Institute for School Reform and other organizations and school districts around the country, has supported thousands of educators in their quest to create better schools for the children and adults who inhabit them. As a part of her work, Gene has masterfully designed multiple protocols that have changed the ways professionals communicate with one another in schools. We have used and adapted many of these protocols in our work with powerful results. We thank Gene, to whom this book is dedicated, for the dedication she has given to making life and learning conditions better for teachers and the children they teach. She continues to influence, inspire, and enrich our growing understandings of learning community work.

In addition to Gene, many outstanding and inspirational educators have developed protocols and generously shared them for use by others to make PLCs stronger across the nation. We describe many of these, available on the SRI website (www.schoolreforminitiative.org) in this book. While not all protocols note their creators (many simply state they were developed by a group of educators), we would like to acknowledge all who have developed these critical resources for teacher professional learning, both the ones we specifically describe in this book as well as the many others that exist. In this book specifically, we reference the following protocols:

- "Forming Ground Rules," developed by Marylyn Wentworth
- "Creating Metaphors," adapted from *The Courage to Teach*, Parker Palmer, pp. 144–150, by Gene Thompson-Grove
- "Group Juggle," developed in the field by educators
- "North, South, East, and West: Compass Points," developed in the field by educators
- "Three Levels of Text Protocol," adapted by the Southern Maine Partnership from Camilla Greene's Rule of 3 Protocol
- "Four 'A's Text Protocol," adapted from Judith Gray, Seattle, Washington (2005)
- "Individual Monthly Action Plan (I-MAP)," developed by Debbie Bambino
- "ATLAS: Looking at Data," developed by Eric Buchovecky based in part on the work of the Leadership for Urban Mathematics Project and Assessment Communities of Teachers Project. It also draws on the work of Steve Seidel and Evangeline Harris-Stefanakis of Project Zero at Harvard University. This protocol was revised by Gene Thompson-Grove (November 2000) and Dianne Leahy (August 2004).
- "Data Driven Dialogue," developed by the Teacher Development Group based on work presented by Nancy Love, author of *Using Data/Getting Results* (2002)
- "Data Mining Protocol," developed in the field by educators in City Schools of Decatur, Georgia
- "Chalk Talk Protocol," developed by Hilton Smith, Foxfire Fund; adapted by Marylyn Wentworth

About the Authors

 **Nancy Fichtman Dana** is currently professor of education in the School of Teaching and Learning at the University of Florida, Gainesville. She began her career in education as an elementary school teacher in Hannibal Central Schools, New York. Since earning her PhD from Florida State University in 1991, she has been a passionate advocate for engaging teachers in powerful job-embedded professional learning and has worked with numerous schools and districts across the nation and abroad to develop inquiry-oriented learning communities as well as conducted much research on inquiry, learning communities, and other forms of job-embedded learning. She has published nine books and over sixty articles in professional journals and edited books focused on teacher and principal professional development. Dana has received many honors, including the Association of Teacher Educator's Distinguished Research in Teacher Education Award and the National Staff Development Council (NSDC) Book of the Year Award, both honoring Dana and Yendol-Hoppey's work related to professional development.

 **Diane Yendol-Hoppey** is the David C. Anchin Endowed Professor, director of the Anchin Center, and the associate dean of Education Preparation and Partnerships at the University of South Florida. Prior to her work in higher education, Diane taught public school for thirteen years in Pennsylvania and Maryland. Diane's work specifically focuses on preservice and in-service teacher learning and leadership through job-embedded professional development. Prior to her current position at the University of South Florida, she held positions at the University of Florida and West Virginia University. In these appointments, she collaborated with practitioners and other university faculty to strengthen and research preservice and in-service teacher learning targeted at school improvement. Her leadership related to

working with schools has facilitated and sustained nationally recognized school/university partnerships. She has coauthored four books as well as published over fifty studies that have appeared in such journals as *Educational Researcher, Teachers College Record,* and *Journal of Teacher Education.*

1

PLC Defined

H‌ave you ever wondered . . .

- Why is teacher professional development often ineffective?
- What would it take to improve teacher professional development?
- What would it take to improve student learning?
- What does professional learning look like that is contextually specific?
- Why can't professional development be more closely related to the problems or dilemmas I face in my classroom?

Have you ever thought . . .

- Why did I just sit in a three-day workshop about something I already know?
- Why did I just sit in a three-day workshop about something that is too difficult to do in my classroom?

Have you ever asked a colleague . . .

- How did you do that?
- Can I have a copy of your . . .?
- What can I do about . . .?

Finally, have you ever looked at an exemplary teacher and wondered why others didn't know the same strategies? If you answered yes to any of these questions, then a professional learning community (PLC) is likely a place for you.

WHAT IS A PLC?

In schools today, teachers seem constantly challenged to solve problems that someone else identifies and implement endless changes advocated by those outside the four walls of the classroom—administrators, politicians, consultants, federal and state departments of education, researchers, and the list goes on and on. While teachers have gained insights into their practices from these groups, teacher voices have typically been absent from these larger conversations about how to approach solving persisting teaching and student learning problems. PLCs, when well done, allow teachers to collaboratively untangle some of the complexities associated with student learning that occur within their school buildings and classrooms. The approach allows educators to proactively solve their own dilemmas rather than waiting for others to mandate solutions to these problems that may or may not be effective or appropriate. In sum, a PLC can be defined as a group of educators who are collaboratively engaged in contextually specific learning by raising questions that are relevant to their local context and working together to answer those questions.

To better understand what a PLC is, it's often useful to start with what a PLC is not. First and foremost, a PLC cannot be delivered as a workshop. For many years, educators have learned what effective professional learning does and does not look like. The research has clearly demonstrated that the "sit and get" workshop model of professional development still exists. In the workshop model, outside experts introduce new strategies, approaches, and pedagogy, and then teachers are expected to return to their classrooms and independently implement the new knowledge. The workshop model, when used in isolation, is not effective in changing classroom practice (Desimone, 2009; Showers & Joyce, 1995).

In contrast, PLCs situate the focus on professional learning within an ongoing community of support. The PLC honors the expertise within the school community. Just like the name entails, PLCs bring groups of educators together to *learn*. Over 40 years ago, Goldhammer (1969) emphasized the need for opportunities to help teachers understand what they are doing and why, by changing schools from places where teachers just act out "age old rituals" to places where teachers participate fully in the learning process for their own professional growth. Nolan and Huber (1989) described successful professional development programs as "making a difference in the lives and instruction of teachers who participate in them, as well as the lives of the students they teach" (p. 143). More recently, in the *Journal of Staff Development*, educators from across the country put forth their vision for "The Road Ahead" for professional learning. These ideas included the importance of creating activities, tools, and contexts that blend theory and practice (Darling-Hammond, 2007); supporting collaborative learning structures that deepen innovation implementation efforts (DuFour & DuFour, 2007); strengthening professionalism by recognizing the complexity and importance of teacher professional knowledge (Elmore, 2007; Hord, 2007; Schlechty, 2007); and making professional learning a part of the work of each teacher in every classroom (Fullan, 2007). Each of these ideas reflects the type of learning that can occur in or from a PLC.

Secondly, a PLC is not a replacement name for a committee meeting, staff meeting, department meeting, team meeting, or the like. In schools, committee meetings, staff meetings, department meetings, and team meetings all serve a purpose and can be an important part of work and life in schools. However, unlike PLCs, these types of meetings do not have a laser-like focus on teacher professional development and student learning as their primary goal and reason for being. Rather, a committee might be formed to accomplish a particular task, such as reviewing and selecting a new textbook series for the school or district, whereas staff, department, and team meetings often function in order to work through logistical aspects of teaching and to ensure the smooth running of a school, department, or grade level.

Unfortunately, in many places across the nation, schools and districts have "jumped on the PLC bandwagon" too quickly and in their haste to actualize the promise PLCs hold have ended up simply renaming already existing structures such as committee, staff, department, and team meetings as "PLCs." When this happens, teachers don't experience the benefits of PLCs and become disenchanted with this mechanism for professional learning. Sadly, in some schools and districts, we have even seen *PLC* be referred to by teachers as a "three-letter dirty word."

Given that many schools are already implementing PLCs, how do you know if your PLC is in name only? Learning Forward (2015), the premier national organization for teacher professional development (formally National Staff Development Council [NSDC]), offers teachers a way to assess whether their PLC is really a PLC. This assessment criteria helps to further define and clarify what a PLC is and what a PLC is not. According to this organization, a well-functioning PLC should do the following:

- evaluate student, teacher, and school learning needs by reviewing data on teacher and school performance;
- define a clear set of educator learning goals based on analysis of data;
- achieve educator learning goals by implementing coherent, sustained, and evidence-based learning strategies that improve instructional effectiveness and student achievement;
- provide job-embedded assistance to help teachers transfer new knowledge and skills to the classroom;
- regularly assess the effectiveness of PLCs in relationship to ongoing improvements in teaching and student learning; and
- request external expertise when the community determines it is needed.

By reviewing these characteristics, you will have a better idea as to whether you're really currently working in a learning community. If your assessment is that the group is not engaged in these activities, then it is time to start rethinking how your community works. This book will help you do that.

In this book, we take a broad and practitioner-driven definition of PLC—one that allows educators not only to participate in the process but also to have a say in the development of the PLC process at their school. In sum, the overarching description of a successful PLC is simple— have robust conversations about improving teaching and learning that includes research, multiple forms of data, teacher knowledge construction, support in between meetings, and public sharing that target and ultimately lead to improved student learning.

DO PLCs REALLY WORK?

At this point, you may be thinking that PLCs sound good in theory, but over time you have developed a healthy skepticism. The everyday work of teaching is already challenging, and teachers are constantly asked to do more and more with less and less. If teachers are to embrace PLCs, it's important to know what evidence exists to show this is really worth doing.

So what evidence exists that PLCs are worth doing? Fortunately, evidence abounds that teachers' participation in well-functioning PLCs is indeed worth the effort (Vescio, Ross, & Adams, 2008). A comprehensive research report on PLCs, conducted by the Southwest Regional Educational Laboratory (2007), identified multiple ways the PLC has demonstrated a positive impact on teachers and their students. The report identifies that PLCs have the power to change school culture, teacher impact, and student achievement. In regards to culture, PLCs cultivate collective responsibility, as well as lead to deprivatization, reflective dialogue, and faculty empowerment. PLCs also have an impact on teachers. For example, Hord (1997) reported decreased teacher isolation and heightened commitment to shared goals and responsibilities. Trimble and Peterson (2000) added that teacher participation in PLCs identified changes in teacher classroom practice, including increased understanding of content taught and roles they play in students' learning. Other research has noted that PLC participation increases teacher renewal, satisfaction, morale, and participation in change.

In addition to PLCs helping change the school's culture and positively affecting teachers, evidence exists that when done right PLCs can enhance student achievement. In general, researchers have identified an important positive relationship between teacher PLCs, teacher instructional practices, and student achievement (Buffman & Hinman, 2006; Erb, 1997; Natkin & Jurs, 2005; Wheelan & Kesselring, 2005; Wheelan & Tilin, 1999). Not surprisingly, these researchers have also reported that the students of teachers who participated in mature PLCs that really focus on student learning performed higher on standardized tests. Students also demonstrated better attitudinal and behavioral outcomes including greater satisfaction, increased commitment to doing school work, and more engagement. All of this evidence suggests the promise and possibility PLC work holds for transforming schools, empowering teachers, and enhancing student learning.

HOW DO PLCs WORK?

PLCs are typically composed of six to twelve educators who meet on a regular basis to systematically and intentionally learn with and from one another about their own teaching practice through engagement in deliberative and purposeful professional dialogue. PLCs serve to connect a group of professionals to do just what their name entails—*learn* from practice. Although PLCs meet on a regular basis, just because they meet doesn't mean that learning happens. Sometimes PLC members understand the end goal of their work to be teacher and student learning, but they may not know how to engage in the type of professional dialogue together that will get them there.

One resource that PLC members can draw upon are protocols. Protocols can ensure focused, deliberate conversation and dialogue by teachers about student work and student learning. McDonald, Mohr, Dichter, and McDonald (2003) explain the importance of using protocols:

> In diplomacy, protocol governs who greets whom first when the President and Prime Minister meet, and other such matters. In technology, protocols enable machines to "talk" with one another by precisely defining the language they use. In science and medicine, protocols are regimens that ensure faithful replication of an experiment or treatment; they tell the scientist or doctor to do this first, then that, and so on. And in social science, they are the scripted questions that an interviewer covers, or the template for an observation. But in the professional education of educators? One could argue that elaborate etiquette, communicative precision, faithful replication, and scripts would prove counterproductive here. Don't we best learn from each other by just talking with each other? No, we claim. Among educators especially, *just* talking may not be enough. The kind of talking needed to educate ourselves cannot rise spontaneously and unaided from *just* talking. It needs to be carefully planned and scaffolded. (p. 4)

Protocols for educators provide a script or series of timed steps for how a conversation among teachers on a chosen topic will develop.

A variety of different protocols have been developed for use in PLCs by a number of noteworthy organizations. While many excellent materials have been produced by numerous organizations, in this book, we rely most heavily on resources from School Reform Initiative (SRI), an organization working to create transformational learning communities fiercely committed to educational equity and excellence. Further information about SRI can be found at www.schoolreforminitiative.org. If you are interested in PLC work and not already a member of SRI, we highly recommend membership to connect you to other professionals across the country that are working to change the nature of the dialogue that happens among the professionals in schools into meaningful and learning-full conversation with the assistance of protocols. We also highly recommend the training SRI provides to fully understand the use of protocols, their purpose, their limitations, and the role they can play in PLC work.

In sum, when used within a PLC, protocols can ensure planned, intentional conversation by teachers within each PLC meeting. The protocols can help teachers identify dilemmas and questions, help teachers become familiar with and review external expertise, help identify the types of data that need to be collected, help teachers analyze student work or a lesson to be taught, lead to new insights and learning, and help point to changes needed in practice. Different protocols are selected for use depending on where the PLC is in its work, what the topic for discussion is at a particular PLC meeting, as well as what the purpose of that discussion is in relationship to moving the work of the PLC forward.

A word of caution regarding protocols is important to note. Because the dialogue and conversation that occurs in education has not been structured traditionally, teachers have had few opportunities to engage in rich professional exchanges with their teaching colleagues. When teachers experience dialogue and conversation that is structured by the use of a protocol like the learning communities you will read about in this book, they are often "blown away" by the richness of their exchange with colleagues. This rich exchange fills an empty void in the teacher's practice that has existed for years, and PLC members express how marvelous a protocol-led discussion has been for their professional learning.

Protocols *can* be very powerful. However, the power of protocols can become seductive when PLC members marvel at how incredible the experience of engaging in dialogue using the protocol has been for them. This can lead some PLCs to believe that the selection and use of protocols is the most important part of their work. PLCs begin planning their meetings around this question: What protocol would be good for our PLC to try this week? rather than What is the next step in our collective work to move us closer to our PLC goals? It's important to remember that the value of protocols is not in the protocols themselves but in their ability to be used by a PLC as a tool to move the PLC group members' collective work forward.

Protocols work for the PLC. The PLC doesn't work for the protocols. It is important that PLCs do not let the use of protocols become more important than the learning of the group.

WHY IS THIS BOOK CALLED *THE PLC BOOK*?

Having read and reviewed in this chapter what PLCs are and are not, what evidence exists to support their implementation, and how PLCs work in general, it may seem like PLCs can be pretty complicated. Hence, you may be wondering, Why is the title of the book so simple? The answer to that question is also simple. PLCs should not be complicated. They should be effective. The structure and process that PLCs use need to be easy to navigate. However, with the proliferation of workshops, books, and materials that have been generated about PLC work by different consultants, authors, and educational scholars in recent years, PLC structure and process has taken on all different shapes and sizes. Special processes and procedures, steps, and rules to guide PLC work have been offered by many, with one approach differing from the next, and often each approach becoming more and more intricate and complicated than the ones offered before. While much can be learned from different approaches and actualizations of PLC work, it can also lead to confusion among teachers who just want to focus on solving dilemmas that they are facing in their classrooms and schools.

Being able to simply navigate the PLC structure and process is particularly important when the problems educators are trying to solve today are *not* simple at all. Linda Darling-Hammond (1997) wisely explains, "Effective teaching is not routine, students are not passive, and questions of practice are not simple, predictable, or standardized" (p. 67). Too many people, both internal and external to schools, have complicated the PLC process, ignoring the simplicity of the learning that many good teachers are naturally inclined do—pose and explore questions about the highly complex act of teaching in an effort to make learning powerful and possible for all the students they serve.

Hence, we wrote this book to bring simplicity back to the PLC process while simultaneously honoring the complexity inherent in teaching itself. We believe PLCs build on effective teachers' natural inclinations to solve the complexity of teaching and that PLC process and procedure can simply mirror that natural inclination, providing space and opportunity for teachers to work collaboratively to

- give voice to issues, tensions, problems and dilemmas they face due to the complexity of teaching;
- decide on which issues, tensions, problems, and dilemmas they wish to focus their gaze;

- develop a plan for how to learn together to gain insights into the area they selected for focus through such activities as reading on the subject and collection and analysis of data;
- implement that plan;
- take action based on their individual and collective learning; and
- share the learning of the PLC with others.

We have organized this book to illustrate the ways teachers' natural inclinations to learn from practice, which was just articulated, can be simply translated into five components of PLC work: "Getting Started" (Chapter 2), "Establishing a PLC Direction" (Chapter 3), "Developing a PLC Action Learning Plan" (Chapter 4), "Analyzing Data in Your PLC" (Chapter 5), and "Making PLC Learning Public" (Chapter 6).

Each of these chapters follows the same format. First, we discuss the "what" and "why" of each component, simply defining each component and explicating the reasons it is important for a PLC to give attention to it. Next, we discuss the "how" of each component, suggesting and providing resources, such as specific protocols PLCs might use when they are at this particular stage in their learning. Next, we articulate what each component of PLC work might look like in practice. Often offered as a story depicting a particular meeting of a PLC, this portion of each chapter allows the reader to become a "fly on the wall" and "observe" a PLC actualizing each component of PLC work. Finally, we end each chapter with questions for discussion, designed to help you and your PLC members unpack each component and apply it to your own PLC work in ways that make sense to you.

The final chapter of the book, titled "Essential Elements of a Healthy PLC," looks across each component of PLC work, naming and discussing ten essential elements of a healthy and highly functioning PLC. While the previous chapters explore individual components of PLC work, this final chapter provides a bird's-eye view of it, offering important considerations to keep in mind as PLCs form and function over time.

Together, we have over fifty years of experience studying and working in schools alongside teachers to actualize powerful professional learning. As a result, in large part, this book was put together by applying work we have done with all different types of teacher-driven, job-embedded forms of professional development to the form and functionality of PLCs. To do so, we borrow from many of our previous writings, drawing most heavily on an award-winning book we wrote for coaches of PLCs in 2009: *The Reflective Educator's Guide to Professional Development: Coaching Inquiry-Oriented Learning Communities*. To write *The PLC Book*, we sought to combine the best of all we have learned about PLCs since that time and write for all members of a PLC, not just one individual who may be considered "the coach." Our goal in the writing of this book was that all members of a PLC would have equal ownership of and insights into the form and functionality of the PLC, with the process being demystified and simply and succinctly explained for all who participate as PLC members.

Whether you are new to PLC work or are currently engaging in PLC work in your school or district, we hope this text provides helpful ideas for you to consider as you begin or renew PLC work currently underway. For although the acts of teaching that are the focus of PLC work are both complicated and complex, the structure and process of PLC work itself need not be. If PLC structure and process becomes terribly complicated, it risks detracting from and even overtaking the purpose of PLCs in the first place—teacher and student *learning*. We hope the content of this book will put *learning* back front and center, where it belongs in a PLC, by providing simple explanations and illustrations of PLC work. Let's get started with an exploration of getting PLC work started, the focus of Chapter 2.

2

Getting Started

WHAT GETTING STARTED
IS AND WHY IT'S IMPORTANT

Getting started in your professional learning community (PLC) consists of forming a small group of colleagues that will constitute your PLC; establishing a regularly scheduled meeting time and place; collectively developing norms that will guide your learning with one another; and building strong, trusting relationships among all PLC members. Ironing out the logistical components of who the members of your PLC will be and when you will meet as well as creating ground rules for your learning together and developing strong relationships provides the structure upon which your work will rest.

While creating PLC structures (figuring out the who, when, and how) is a critical first step to PLC work—perhaps the most difficult and time consuming work in getting started is developing relationships. Relationship building is difficult in schools for a myriad of reasons, including teachers being used to spending the bulk of their day alone in a classroom without other adult interaction (see, for example, Lieberman & Miller, 1992) and the congenial nature of many schools that might artificially hide the need to focus time and attention on relationship development.

Congeniality refers to the friendly, cordial relationships some teachers have with one another in the workplace. We see congeniality when teachers chat in the lunchroom about weekend plans, last night's basketball game, or the latest episode of *The Voice*. We might also engage in congeniality when attending birthday celebrations or retirement parties as well as sharing resources. According to Roland Barth (1990), congeniality is defined as "people enjoying each other's company" (p. 30).

Although PLCs need congeniality, congeniality does not alone promote teacher learning and professional knowledge construction. The dialogue that occurs in a purely congenial relationship excludes the kind of teacher talk that promotes wondering, thought, challenge, growth, and action. The type of relationship that allows conversation that promotes professional knowledge construction is *collegiality*. Barth (2006) shares the following:

> Famous baseball manager Casey Stengel once muttered, "Getting good players is easy. Getting 'em to play together is the hard part." Schools are full of good players. Collegiality is about getting them to play together, about growing a professional learning community. (p. 22)

Collegiality moves beyond congeniality and defines the type of relationship that is needed for powerful and meaningful PLC work to unfold.

Judith Warren Little (1981) offers insight into four specific behaviors that characterize the conditions of collegial work. First, she emphasizes that adults in the school must have frequent, continuous, concrete, and precise *talk about their teaching practice.* Second, she emphasizes the importance of adults in schools *observing each other* engaged in the practice of teaching and administration and serving as critical friends to each other as they talk about those observations. Third, she describes the importance of teachers collaboratively *working on curriculum* by planning, designing, researching, and evaluating their curriculum work. Finally, Judith Warren Little discusses that adults in schools must become comfortable sharing their new craft knowledge by *teaching each other* what they have learned. Each of these activities is key to PLC work and requires explicit attention by all PLC members.

As a member of a PLC, you will need to realize that early PLC work requires establishing ways of being together that are often quite different than the typical cultural milieu of the school. As your PLC work unfolds, you will most likely face challenges that will cause you to reflect, ponder, and even wonder if you should retreat before you eventually resolve the challenge and move forward. The establishment of strong, trusting *collegial* relationships between all PLC members is the glue that will hold the PLC together during challenging times. But these challenging times are precisely what helps you surface, confront, and interrogate your own teaching practice together in the name of making teaching and learning conditions better for all the learners you teach. It is the development of strong, trusting collegial relationships that will ultimately make the work of the PLC worthwhile. Time invested in relationship development at the start of (and throughout) the PLC work is a necessary endeavor.

HOW TO GET STARTED

There are many different ways to configure membership of a PLC. Some PLCs form from existing structures such as academic departments or grade level teams who already have a regularly scheduled meeting time established but wish to remake that meeting time from the traditional focus on addressing department- or grade-level administrative particulars to powerful job-embedded professional learning and improvement for all members of the department or team. Some PLCs form based on a common felt need or difficulty several teachers are experiencing and wish to explore together. Some PLCs form based on the congenial and collegial relationships some teachers may have already established with one another, and they simply desire to formalize these relationships and deepen them through a PLC structure. Some PLCs form out of members' desire to reduce the isolation they feel as a classroom teacher. And, while not optimal, some PLCs form based on school or district mandates. All PLC formation structures (even those that are mandated) share benefits and drawbacks, as sometimes mandated PLCs, if coupled with appropriate administrative support, can provide the pressure that is needed to begin this powerful form of professional learning. However you find membership in a PLC, the work of your PLC will occur during a regularly scheduled meeting time.

Just as there are many ways to configure membership in a PLC, there are many different configurations for the frequency and duration of PLC meetings. Your decision regarding how often and how long to meet will be dependent on multiple factors including available time all PLC members have in common given other professional and personal commitments. Some PLCs meet on a weekly or bimonthly basis for approximately one hour for each meeting. Other PLCs meet once a month for a longer period of time. Regardless of how often and how long you meet, it will be important from the start of your work to match your expectations for your PLC to the amount of time you can devote to it. For the work of a PLC to be worthwhile, we recommend a *minimum* of 75 to 120 minutes of meeting time a month (one meeting of this length or two 45–60 minute meetings). We also recommend that you establish a commitment to engaging in some PLC activity in between meetings. This in-between work keeps the PLC work at the forefront and moving forward toward your shared goals.

At the very first meeting of your PLC, it will be important to develop norms for your learning together. This can be accomplished by engaging in some variation of a protocol called "Forming Ground Rules (Creating Norms)" developed by Marylyn Wentworth (http://schoolreforminitia tive.org/doc/forming_ground_rules.pdf). This protocol involves each member of the PLC articulating what he or she needs from the group to be able to do his or her best work. The list of needs generated by the group is then discussed, and similar items may be combined to whittle down the entire list to a manageable length. This list becomes the "ground rules" or "community agreements" for PLC work moving forward and is reviewed at the start of each PLC meeting.

There are a number of protocols available from the School Reform Initiative (SRI) that help PLC members get to know one another professionally in ways that don't ordinarily occur in everyday interactions between faculty members. Some of our favorite professional relationship building protocols include the "Creating Metaphors" protocol (http:// schoolreforminitiative.org/doc/creating_metaphors.pdf), "Group Juggle," (http://schoolreforminitiative.org/doc/group_juggle.pdf), and "Compass Points: North, South, East, and West" (http://schoolreforminitiative.org/doc/compass_points.pdf). Building relationships can occur through the implementation of protocols such as those just named as a part of PLC meetings (with heavier focus on relationship building early in the PLC formation). In addition, a short five-minute opening activity or sharing time instituted at the start of every PLC meeting where all PLC members whip around and share their response to a prompt is a great way to weave relationship building into every meeting. Prompts could be random in nature; correspond to the current work of the PLC; or simply correspond to times in the calendar year, such as "As we begin a new school year, share one thing you are looking most forward to about your work as a teacher this year," or "For our February PLC meeting, since this is the month of Valentine's Day, let's reconnect with each other today by sharing the one thing we love most about teaching."

Planning and facilitation of the first and subsequent PLC meetings can be assigned to one member of the PLC (who may have received training from an organization like SRI), or it may rotate through all members of the PLC, with different members taking the responsibility for planning and leading each meeting.

WHAT DOES GETTING STARTED LOOK LIKE?

We illustrate what getting started might look like through a fictitious PLC meeting that is based on a composite of actual PLC initial meetings we have participated in or observed ourselves. The meeting in this illustration occurs in a newly formed PLC that consists of eight members at an elementary school—the reading coach (Cara) and seven additional teachers from different grade levels within the building who formulated their PLC based on a shared concern for the ways their reading instruction needed to change due to the adoption of the Common Core State Standards. The eight women in this group all knew one another and had been talking about their concern related to implementation of the Common Core State Standards. They decided to meet after school on the first Monday of every month from 3:00 to 5:00. With support from their principal, each member of the PLC would receive professional development points needed for state licensure for participating in this professional development endeavor. Having participated in SRI training, the reading coach took responsibility for facilitating the first meeting of the group, planning the group's activities in consultation with all members of the PLC. They decided for their initial meeting that they would agree to meet for an additional thirty minutes (two and one-half hours total) to develop a solid foundation for and kickoff of their PLC work.

Knowing the importance of building relationships, Cara began this group's initial meeting with a five-minute opening activity where each member of the group shared one hope and one fear they had about what the Common Core State Standards would mean to their reading instruction. As a transition from this opening activity, Cara stated that what will bind members of the PLC together in their work ahead is their shared hopes and fears related to adopting the Common Core.

Another aspect of binding the group together will be really knowing deeply who each other is professionally so they can help one another navigate the Common Core and integrate these new standards seamlessly into their practice. Hence, Cara introduced the SRI protocol designed to help the teachers in this PLC begin to open up to each other about professional challenges as well as discover things about their identities as teachers through composing and sharing a metaphor that describes their teaching. Cara reviewed the steps to the "Creating Metaphors" protocol (http://schoolreforminitiative.org/doc/creating_metaphors.pdf) that began with each teacher completing this statement: When I am at my best as a teacher, I am _____. Next, Cara directed the group to draw a picture, symbol, or some other graphic representation of the metaphor they selected to complete the statement. She also asked them to jot down a few sentences that describe the guidance this metaphor offers them in tough or sticky situations as well as to reflect on the "shadows" inherent in their metaphor.

When everyone in the group had finished writing, each PLC member proceeded to share their metaphors with one another. Amid some laughter and teasing, Tara volunteered to speak first, "I am a surfer, always awake to the hazards, but excited and enjoying life. I ride the waves of the classroom with all the ups and downs. No matter how out of control it gets, I always go back for more in search of that perfect ride." Delia joined in, "I am an astronaut. My students and I have different types of knowledge, and we must work as a team on the mission of learning and discovering. Like a mission, sometimes my students lead, sometimes I chart our course, and sometimes we get 'lost in space' as we attempt to go where no one has ever gone before."

After the remaining members of the learning community shared their metaphors, Cara facilitated the further discussion of each metaphor by asking the learning community members to discuss both the strengths and shadows of each metaphor in turn. After a learning community member's metaphor was discussed by the group, Cara returned the conversation to the teacher who presented the metaphor and asked her to discuss what parts of the strengths and shadows discussion resonated with her teaching experience. After all metaphors had been presented and discussed, Cara debriefed the activity in two steps: asking the learning community members to share what they learned about each other and asking the learning community members how they might do something similar with their students. Although these women were good friends and collegial with each other, Cara knew they were venturing into a new professional relationship as they worked to establish a PLC. Cara's immediate goal for utilizing this metaphor activity during the first part of their initial meeting was to reinforce the trust these teachers had in each other while refocusing their relationship around professional issues.

Following the metaphor activity, the group moved to establishing the norms for their PLC. Cara asked each member of the PLC to think about and list on a piece of paper what they need from this group, from each other, in order to do their very best work when they are at their once a month PLC meetings. Cara gave the example of honoring the busy lives they all have as teachers, so for her to do her best work, she was going to write down "Start our meetings on time."

In response, one PLC member chimed in, "I know what you mean, but how about *ending* meetings on time too? Nothing gets me more agitated than when I need to get home to my kids and a meeting ends up running over."

With the example of "Start and end meetings on time," articulated, everyone had five minutes of silence to jot down items on their list. Next, Cara asked each PLC member in round-robin fashion to share one item on her list with the group and noted the item on chart paper. The first four items Cara wrote were "Start and end meetings on time," "Silence cell phones to be fully present at the meeting," "Be honest and open with one another," and "Monitor the amount of time you talk during each meeting. Listen to others twice as much as you speak."

The next item was contributed by Tara, who shared, "We teach in a small community where everyone knows all about each other. We need to be able to talk openly at our meetings without fear that our words will be repeated widely around the school and in the town. I think that we have to agree that what we say in these meetings stays in these meetings."

All of the teachers nodded in agreement, and Cara smiled as she summarized this comment with the phrase "Vegas Rules" on the chart paper, chuckling aloud, "You know that old saying 'What happens in Vegas stays in Vegas.' Well, we can't afford a trip to Vegas—although I sure would like to go—but we can use that saying as a code to remind us all that what we share about ourselves, our teaching, and our students does not get discussed anywhere other than in our meetings. Vegas Rules is code for 'What happens in our PLC stays in our PLC.'"

A next suggestion was particularly important for this group of eight women who knew each other for a number of years and had strong congenial relationships with one another, "Since we're talking code here, could we add another one? How about Q-TIP? Q-TIP stands for 'Quit taking it personally.' This ground rule was established in a learning community I was a member of previously. Because we all know each other well, conversations can easily veer from professional to personal within the same sentence. Q-TIP will remind us that our work during these meetings is about student and teacher learning—it is not about anyone's *personal* lives. Rather, it's about getting better at the work we do in our *professional* lives." All of the teachers nodded their heads in agreement, and Cara added Q-TIP (Quit taking it personally and stay focused on our students) on the chart.

After everyone exhausted every item on the list, the group discussed the list as a whole, combined and reworded a few entries, and deleted one item they couldn't all agree to abide by; then their community agreements were formed. Cara shared she would rewrite the norms neatly on a fresh sheet of chart paper and hang them up at each meeting as a reminder of the PLC way of working with each other.

Cara transitioned to the next component of the PLC meeting by saying, "In addition to the agreements we just made about the way we will work with one another, it will also be really important for us all to share the same basic understanding of PLC work, what it is, and what we are trying to accomplish as a group. To achieve this goal, let's spend a little time unpacking what a PLC is by reading a short piece, an oldie but a goodie, called 'Building Professional Community in Schools' by Sharon Kruse, Karen Seashore Louis, and Anthony Bryk (1994), and use a protocol to help us process this article."

For those PLC members who weren't familiar with protocols, Cara defined what they were and shared with the group they had already used two in their meeting that afternoon—one called "Creating Metaphors" to help them deepen their professional relationships and one called "Forming Ground Rules" to help them develop the agreements they just made. Cara explained that another type of protocol is referred to as "Text-Based Discussion Protocols," which help a PLC unpack and make sense of a reading together. She then provided an example of two they would use for the remaining time of their first meeting, called "Three Levels of Text Protocol" (http://schoolreforminitiative.org/doc/3_levels_text.pdf) and "Four 'A's Text Protocol" (http://schoolreforminitiative.org/doc/4_a_text.pdf) to discuss both the "Building Professional Community in Schools" reading and a second reading on the topic that brought the PLC together in the first place—the Common Core State Standards.

Before this first meeting, the group had decided that one thing they needed to do as a PLC was to develop knowledge about the Common Core. Prior to the meeting, they selected and ordered a book from one of their favorite authors on the teaching of reading: Lucy Calkins. *Pathways to the Common Core* (Calkins, Ehrenworth, & Lehman, 2012) would be used as a resource for their PLC work, and all members of the PLC agreed to read the first chapter of this text before their first meeting. Cara asked them to come to the first meeting having identified four passages in the text in four different categories: a passage they agreed with, a passage they wished to argue with, a passage they wished to aspire to, and a passage they wanted to take action on.

When planning this first PLC meeting, Cara wrestled with whether she should have the eight group members read the articles ahead of time or if she should devote time during the meeting to reading the articles. She believed it would take about eight to ten minutes for the group to read "Building Professional Community in Schools" and fifteen to twenty minutes to read the first chapter of the Calkins et al. (2012) book. Not wanting to spend too large a proportion of their first meeting together in silent reading time, she decided that the group would read the short "Building Professional Community in Schools" piece at the meeting itself and asked the group to come to the meeting having read the first chapter of *Pathways to the Common Core*.

Cara distributed "Building Professional Community in Schools," along with the "Three Levels of Text Protocol" to each PLC member. She noted that the protocol would help them focus their reading and that part of the protocol asked the members to identify passages in the text as they read that they believed had important implications for defining the PLC work. She then gave the group about 10 minutes to read the article.

Once they finished reading, Cara reviewed the protocol instructions. The group would divide into two smaller groups of four members each and sit in two small circles to engage in "rounds." A round consisted of group members taking turns sharing one of their highlighted excerpts from the article and reflecting on what that excerpt meant to them, followed by the group responding (for a total of up to two minutes) to what has been said. Delia was the first volunteer. Delia began her three minutes of reflection by reading the passage she had selected and sharing how she interpreted the passage as well as how her interpretations connected and disconnected with her own past professional development activities. She then described the implications she believed the passage had for defining their PLC. After listening carefully, the group spent two minutes responding to her reflection. This process continued until all group members had shared using the same processing format.

Once everyone in the four-member group had shared, the entire PLC got back together and took about five minutes to synthesize what they had learned about PLC work from the article and then they debriefed the protocol process. This activity allowed the group to create some shared understandings about PLCs through focused dialogue. The debriefing process also allowed the group to critique the protocol process. Agreeing that protocols worked really well to keep the group focused on the text, they turned to the second text-based discussion protocol called "The Four 'A's Text Protocol" to guide their conversation about the first chapter of the Calkins et al. (2012) text.

As a reminder, members of the learning community had come to this first meeting both having read the first chapter of this book as well as having highlighted one passage each in the text that answered the following four questions:

- What do you **agree** with in the text?
- What do you want to **argue** with in the text?
- What part of the text do you want to **aspire** to?
- What **actions** does this text inspire you to take?

As she explained this protocol, Cara once again asked the PLC to get back into their four-person groups. She then explained that each group would begin a series of rounds talking about the text in light of each of the As, beginning with agreements and then taking the other three As one at a time. Each member of the group would have one minute to share about each of the four As in turn. This allowed the PLC members to respond to the article in a small setting, as well as ensuring that every PLC member would participate in the discussion, and no one PLC member would dominate. As the discussion unfolded, teachers had the opportunity to honestly "hear" and understand their colleagues' perspectives. This was a critical first step to professional learning and collaboration.

At the end of all four rounds, Cara led a general discussion focused on this question: What does this reading mean for the work ahead of us related to teaching reading with the Common Core State Standards? The group debriefed the activity by identifying how they might improve their discussions of text in the future as well as what their next steps would be toward focusing on their own professional development as PLC members for the coming school year. They discussed the need to use their next meeting to get a better understanding of the standards themselves and with that understanding further define the work of their PLC by developing one or more guiding questions to focus their learning at each PLC meeting. To accomplish this goal, the members of the group "jigsawed" the four chapters related to the reading standards of the Calkins et al. (2012) text. Two PLC members each agreed to read one of the chapters, and working together, each duo would prepare and provide a ten-minute overview of their chapter for the group at their next PLC meeting. The remaining time at their next meeting would be used to look across the four chapters and develop a specific goal for the PLC work as it continued. Delia volunteered to plan and lead that next meeting as Cara ended their first meeting by asking each PLC member to complete this sentence: One thing I'm looking forward to about the work that lies ahead for this PLC is _____.

The meeting time had gone quickly, and a summary of the day's PLC timeline follows:

3:00   Opening: Whip Around—Share one hope and one fear you have for the Common Core State Standards.

3:10   "Creating Metaphors" protocol

3:35   "Forming Ground Rules" protocol

3:55   Silent reading of article titled "Building Professional Community in Schools"

4:05   Discussion of "Building Professional Community in Schools" article using "Three Levels of Text Protocol"

4:35   Discussion of Chapter 1 of *Pathways to the Common Core* using "The Four 'A's Text Protocol"

5:10   Planning the next steps for PLC work

5:20   Closing: Whip Around—Each member shares her completion of this sentence stem: One thing I'm looking forward to about the work that lies ahead for this PLC is _____.

As the eight members of this PLC walked to the parking lot, they shared with one another how much they accomplished during their first meeting. They mentioned how refreshing it was to set goals, plan, and work together on a topic that they identified. They looked forward to their second meeting next month.

Questions for Discussion

1. Judith Warren Little defines four components of collegial work in schools: (1) frequent, continuous, concrete, and precise talk about teaching practice; (2) observing others engaged in the practice of teaching; (3) working on curriculum by planning, designing, researching, and evaluating curriculum work; and (4) sharing craft knowledge by teaching others what you have learned.

   - Which of these four components were present in the first meeting of this PLC, and how were they achieved?
   - In what ways might the components that were not present in this first meeting be integrated into the future work of this PLC?

2. Using the following chart as a guide, discuss the ways this first PLC meeting was the same as and different from typical committee meetings that occur in a school.

	Committee	*Learning Community*
Purpose	Specific dilemma to be solved	Shared desire for professional development guide purpose
Duration	Ends when purpose is reached	Ongoing cycle of self-study
Focus	Concern for teacher participation in resolution	Concern for member changes in practice
Process	Decision-oriented	Reflection-oriented
Leadership	Designated leader/ chairperson	Facilitator/shared responsibility
Tone	Formal	Informal
Use of Data	Focus on identified need	Focus on student data
Roles	Constant	Shifting
Structure	Traditional meeting structure/hierarchical	Democratic meeting structure/ team-based
Goals	Specific goals from onset	Goals evolve from collaborative study
Time	Bounded time period	Ongoing
Feeling	"Worker bees"	Ownership
Individual/ Group	Consensus needed	Individual voice encouraged
Time	Meet as needed	Continuous

3. Cara used a number of different protocols for different purposes to structure the dialogue that occurred in this first PLC meeting (i.e., "Creating Metaphors," "Forming Ground Rules," "Three Levels of Text Protocol," "The Four 'A's Text Protocol")

   - Which one of these protocols would you feel most comfortable using yourself and why?
   - How and when could you use this protocol in your own PLC work?
   - Which of these protocols would you feel least comfortable using yourself and why?
   - When and why might you use this protocol in your own PLC work, and what, if anything, might help you become more comfortable with its use?

4. The first PLC meeting of the group described in this chapter was two-and-a-half hours in duration.

- How would you redistribute the way time was used in this meeting if the group had agreed to meet twice in their first month for seventy-five minutes each time? (Within this new time frame, are there activities you would rework, delete, and/or add to accomplish the same outcomes?)
- In your opinion, what is the *optimal* amount of time needed for PLC members to meet each month for the work to be of value? In what ways, if any, does your response to this question differ from what you believe to be a *reasonable* amount of time to ask PLC members to meet each month as well as spend time preparing for their next meeting?
- Using the following chart as a guide, discuss various ways to find the time needed in schools for teachers to engage in meaningful PLC work.

   o Which of the strategies in the chart does your school or district already use?
   o Which of the strategies in the chart are unrealistic for use in your school or district?
   o Which of the strategies in the chart might be possible to achieve in your school or district, and how might you initiate a discussion on how to achieve it?

CREATIVE USES OF TIME AND RESOURCES

Restructured Time: Strategies for rearranging time within the teacher contracted school day

- Having early student release or late start for students (where students are sent home early or arrive later one day a week or month)
- Adding more and regularly scheduled professional development days within the school calendar
- Providing teachers who work together a common planning time on a weekly basis
- Extending the school day on four days of the week and dismissing earlier on the fifth day
- Extracting time from existing schedule by taking a few minutes from each period to create an extra planning period for teachers
- Block scheduling to provide longer periods of release time for teachers
- Extending the school calendar to allow for a critical mass of professional development days at the beginning and end of the school year

Staff Time: Strategies that alter the ways staff are utilized

- Making better use of the adults in your building who are not teachers (i.e., paraprofessionals, college interns, parents, community volunteers, and administrators)
- Instituting "Specialist Days." Specialist days are full days where students rotate through their media, art, music, computer, and physical education specials for an entire day, freeing up time for classroom teachers to meet.

Released Time: Strategies that "release" teachers during the contracted school day from other responsibilities so that they may engage in PLC work

- Creating a bank of substitute hours teachers could "cash in" to use for their professional development needs
- Requiring all students to be involved in a certain number of community service hours over the course of a school year. While students are out earning community service hours, teachers can meet.
- Hiring part-time permanent substitute(s) whose job is to rotate through the school releasing teachers when needed to attend to professional development needs
- Developing an intentional, systematic extracurricular event or activity provided by the community so that students would engage in a wide range of meaningful programming that supplements the curriculum while teachers work on school improvement
- Create partner classrooms by teaming different subject area classes (in middle and high school) and different grade-level classrooms (in elementary school). Teachers in partner classrooms take turns taking responsibility for a designated amount of time for the other teachers' classroom along with their own classroom, engaging in a meaningful curricular experience for the double-sized class of students.
- Using large classes for special topics, create independent study for students, or substitute appropriate television or video programming occasionally for regular instruction

Purchased Time: Refers to providing incentives for teachers to spend time outside of the contractual day (weekends, afterschool, summer work) to engage in inquiry

- Providing monetary incentives
- Earning continuing certification hours needed for professional license renewal or graduate credits if a district partners with a college or university
- Trading time (i.e., trading a Saturday workday and getting the day before a holiday off)

(Continued)

(Continued)

• Trading requirements (i.e., for tenured teachers, trading participation in the annual observation/conference/evaluation cycle with the administrator with a more meaningful production of a teacher learning portfolio that captures evidence related to the teacher and his or her students' growth over the course of the school year)
Better Used Time: Strategies for reconceptualizing meeting times that are already in place but may not be currently utilized to their fullest potential • Holding faculty meetings • Having The Grade-Level Team Meeting (in elementary and middle schools) and The Department Meeting (in high schools) • Having a Teacher Work Day
Technology Time: Refers to utilizing some of the latest technology to make it easier for teachers to meet and engage in professional discussion and learning • Using online discussion forums • Blogging, Twittering, and participating in Facebook groups • Videoconferencing

Source: Adapted from Yendol-Hoppey and Dana (2010).

3

Establishing a PLC Direction

WHAT ESTABLISHING A PLC DIRECTION IS AND WHY IT'S IMPORTANT

Establishing the direction of your professional learning community (PLC) consists of coming to a consensus about the focus and direction of your work for the school year and formulating a guiding question. Capturing the focus and direction of your PLC work in the form of a question serves many purposes. First, questions inherently stimulate thinking and the pondering of practice, which are the foundational aspects of PLC work. Second, questions invite wonder about how the teaching and learning conditions in one's classroom or school could be different and, ultimately, improved upon. The importance of wondering together as PLC members and capturing that wondering as an explorable question is best summarized by the famous quote by Socrates: "Wisdom begins in wonder." Creating a space at PLC meetings to wonder together leads to articulation of the wisdom of practice you already have and will continue to develop. Finally, questions often spark more questions, keeping the learning of a PLC rich and vibrant over time.

Not all questions are created equal, however. Teachers, who use questions on a daily basis to frame student learning, know that there are several types of questions (i.e., fact/recall, comprehension, application, analysis, synthesis, evaluation) and use different types of questions for different purposes throughout the teaching day. A simple fact/recall question would not be the right type of question to guide the learning of a PLC over time. Rather, in order to invite, frame, and provide rich and vibrant direction for a PLC, PLC guiding questions must contain certain characteristics, summarized here:

Good PLC Guiding Questions are questions that

- all PLC members are passionate about exploring,
- focus the group's gaze on student learning and student work,
- explore the practice of PLC members rather than trying to change the practice of others,
- are genuine (PLC members don't already know the answer), and
- are open-ended and invite exploration.

Good Guiding Question Characteristic One: Passion

Teaching is complex and demanding work. Engaging in the act of teaching while simultaneously carefully and critically exploring it with colleagues can be challenging at times. For this reason, it's important that all PLC members are passionate about the direction of the PLC work. Being passionate about your PLC guiding question will provide you the energy needed to sustain the PLC work over time.

Good Guiding Question
Characteristic Two: Focus on Student Learning

The target goal for everything one does as a teacher is student learning. However, because the complexity of teaching springs forth many possibilities for PLC exploration, sometimes questions may arise from the group that aren't directly related to student learning and may instead focus on such things as behavior management and time management. While things like behavior management and time management can certainly play a huge role in the classroom and are worthy topics for PLC exploration, it's always important to be sure that the guiding question the group is posing in some way relates back to *student learning* so that, as PLC members, you never lose sight of your target goal when so many factors are competing for your attention. This will enable your PLC to actualize one of the most powerful aspects of PLC work—wrapping the learning of teachers around the learning of students.

Good Guiding Question
Characteristic Three: Focus on PLC Members' Own Practice

When a group of teachers get together to talk about teaching, it is not uncommon for their talk to turn rather quickly in a negative direction. Because teaching is such a complicated endeavor, it is consequently full of challenges, and these challenges can easily turn faculty room and parking lot talk into unproductive venting and complaining sessions. While everyone needs a good venting space from time to time, a PLC is not the place for venting and complaining about the frustrations of one's teaching context, as this can lead to the development of guiding questions that are focused *outside* of the control of the PLC. PLC members who focus *outside* strive to change or control others (administrators, teaching colleagues, or even students themselves) rather than focus their work on student learning within their own teaching practice. The problem with a PLC direction that is focused *outward* on changing the actions and behaviors of others is that the actions of others are outside of each PLC member's control. An important premise of professional development through PLC work is that the only person a teacher can "control" or "change" is himself or herself. PLCs that focus on changing the behavior of others rarely lead to the important self-discoveries about teaching that PLC work can reveal. However, when PLC work *is* focused inward and reveals important insights about student learning that is subsequently shared with others within and outside your school, it can often serendipitously lead to positive change in the behavior of administrators, teaching colleagues, and/or students themselves. Looking outward, however, cannot be the intent of the PLC work from the start. PLC work must focus on members' own classroom practice and members' own students.

Good Guiding Question Characteristic Four: Genuine

When teachers begin PLC work for the first time, it is not uncommon to start in a comfortable place. For example, many times groups focus attention on a pedagogical innovation that PLC members have found success with in the past and have enthusiastically embraced already. Teachers often begin in their comfort zone because it feels safe, and perhaps even empowering, to have the opportunity to discuss and document some of the great teaching and learning that is occurring in the classroom. However, if a PLC stays on this path, it risks investing time and energy into work that will merely confirm something PLC members already know and not lead to any new discoveries about teaching. Therefore, it's important for a guiding question to be real—a question sincerely felt by all members of the PLC and that PLC members do not already have significant insights into or know the answer to before the work of the PLC has even begun.

Good Guiding Question
Characteristic Five: Phrased as Open Ended

As previously stated, one of the major reasons to engage in PLC work is because teaching and learning are inherently complex activities. Because teaching and learning are so complex, it's often counterproductive to develop a guiding question for a PLC that requires a simple yes or no answer. PLC members are not after solely finding out *if* a particular act of teaching works, but *how*, *for whom*, and *under what conditions* a particular act of teaching works. PLC members are even interested in "troubling teaching" by exploring what it means for something to work in the first place. Hence, to honor the great complexity inherent in teaching, a good PLC guiding question is worded in an open-ended manner rather than in a dichotomous (yes or no) fashion.

HOW TO ESTABLISH
A DIRECTION FOR YOUR PLC

Good PLC guiding questions don't emerge without effort—it takes time, thought, and often "playing" with the wording of a question to establish a strong direction for your PLC. PLC guiding questions emerge in several ways, including (1) from PLC-shared readings on a topic, (2) from activity the PLC has engaged in over time, (3) from data, and (4) from protocols designed specifically to evoke questions of practice.

From PLC Readings About a Topic

A PLC may form initially as all members wish to explore a specific topic, such as the PLC described in Chapter 1 where members came together to investigate the Common Core State Standards and what these standards would mean for their teaching of reading. When a PLC begins with a general topic for pursuit in mind, early PLC activity often includes the reading of literature related to the topic and unpacking that literature. The group may use a text-based protocol, such as "Three Levels of Text Protocol" or the "Four 'A's Text Protocol." Even if a PLC forms without a specific topic area for exploration, early PLC activity often includes the reading and debriefing of texts using text-based protocols.

The intentional and systematic discussion of readings using protocols can naturally lead to the formation of a PLC question. For example, a cross-subject area PLC that consisted of all ninth-grade teachers at a small high school originally formed to investigate the achievement gap with particular attention to students who lived in poverty. Their PLC meetings began with several discussions of readings related to closing the achievement gap. One article they selected and read together was titled "Closing the Achievement Gap Through Teacher Collaboration: Facilitating Multiple Trajectories of Teacher Learning," published in *Journal of Advanced Academics* (Levine & Marcus, 2007). Using a protocol called "Save the Last Word for ME" (http://schoolreforminitiative.org/doc/save_last_word .pdf) to discuss this piece, the learning community members discovered that four of the six members had selected the exact same passage from the article as "their most significant":

> Secondary teachers generally see their role as subject-area specialist responsible for contacting parents only if there are problems in their specific class, rather than as resources aiming to engage and partner with families.

As this passage resonated so strongly with all members of the PLC, the group began to discuss their limited focus on parent involvement at the high school level to date and subsequently began to explore ideas for the ways parents might become partners in and resources for student learning. As a result of this discussion, this PLC formulated this guiding question: How can we engage parents at the secondary level as partners in their students' learning, and what difference, if any, does it make to student learning and achievement in all of the subject areas we teach? This question provided direction for the group's learning over the next several months as they engaged in additional readings on the subject and planned, implemented, and assessed numerous strategies to engage parents and examine the resulting impact of parent engagement on student work and student learning.

From Activity the PLC Has Engaged in Over Time

A second way PLC guiding questions might be born is through looking closely at PLC work documentation tools utilized over time. One documentation tool we have observed numerous PLCs use is the "Individual Monthly Action Plan (I-MAP)" (http://schoolreforminitia tive.org/doc/imap.pdf). Members of a PLC complete a monthly action plan individually or collectively at the close of a PLC meeting. The purpose of the I-MAP is to translate the learning that has occurred during a PLC meeting into teachers' practice and to provide continuity from one meeting to the next. Each individual or the entire group states a planned change they will make in practice based on what they learned from the PLC work during that meeting. Then, four columns are completed as teachers answer these questions: (1) Why am I planning to do this? (2) How will I initiate this change? (3) What supports do I need to be successful? and (4) How will I know if I've made progress? The I-MAP form is available on the School Reform Initiative (SRI) website (http://schoolreforminitiative.org/doc/imap.pdf). Looking at the I-MAPs the group completed over time can lead toward some powerful discussions about potential guiding questions.

From Data

A third way PLC guiding questions might develop is from examination of data. For example, all of the six mathematics teachers responsible for teaching Algebra I at a large high school had formed a PLC to support one another in the teaching of this subject, now a requirement for high school graduation in their state. Early in their PLC work, they analyzed their students' performance on last year's end-of-course exam, a state test students must pass to receive course credit for Algebra I. In viewing an item analysis of test questions and responses, they identified two areas of the Algebra I curriculum where their students were not performing as well as they were in other areas of the curriculum: exponents and monomials as well as quadratic equations. As a result of this discovery, this PLC developed this question: In what ways can the units we teach on exponents and monomials and quadratic equations be improved to foster deeper student procedural and conceptual understanding of these concepts in Algebra I?

From Protocols Designed
Specifically to Evoke Questions of Practice

A fourth way PLC guiding questions might develop is as a direct result of engagement in protocols. Many protocols have been specifically designed to help PLC participants give voice to issues, tensions, problems, or dilemmas of practice they are experiencing. These protocols also help participants wonder about the ways these issues, tensions, problems, or dilemmas of practice might be investigated and resolved. For example, our good colleague and PLC coach, Pete Bermudez, created a protocol for exploration with teachers in their PLC work to do just that. In this protocol, teachers read paragraph profiles of eight passions (the student, the curriculum, specific content knowledge, teaching strategies, the relationship between beliefs and practice, the relationship between personal and professional identities, social justice issues, or the importance of context) and select the passion that most accurately describes who they are as an educator. Next, teachers identify others in the room that have identified the same passion, and discuss what it is like to have this passion. After that, each person in the group privately identifies an actual student, by name, who has been affected by the group's profile and writes responses to the following questions:

- What have I done with this student?
- What's worked? What hasn't?
- What else could I do?
- What questions does this raise for me?

After this silent individual writing time, group members discuss the questions that teachers who share this passion are likely to have about their practice. A recorder lists these questions on newsprint, with the passion profile number at the top of the newsprint page.

After briefly hearing reports by each group and viewing the questions generated by each group on newsprint, Pete leads a discussion based on the following questions:

- What strikes you as you listen to the passions of these educators?
- Which of the questions generated intrigues you the most? Why? How might you go about exploring this question with colleagues? What would you do first?

You can adapt the protocol Pete developed and use it at one of your PLC meetings to help stimulate thinking about potential PLC guiding questions. This protocol and the passion profile descriptions appear in Figures 3.1 and 3.2.

Before using this protocol to establish a direction for your PLC, however, it is important to note that while some PLCs establish a single question to guide their learning together (such as the example shared earlier in this chapter: How can we engage parents at the secondary level as partners in their students' learning, and what difference, if any, does it make to student learning and achievement in all of the subject areas we teach?), some PLCs develop an overarching question that captures the direction of their collective work but also develop related subquestions that different individuals or subsets of individuals explore and share with the group to contribute to a greater and richer understanding of the collective PLC question.

For example, a PLC consisting of three fourth-grade teachers at one elementary school and the special education teacher formed with the goal of shifting their regularly scheduled weekly grade-level meetings (that focused mostly on logistical aspects of their work as a grade-level team) to PLC meetings that would focus on analysis of student work and student learning. Over time, the direction for their PLC work emerged as the group engaged in analysis of data reflecting their students' performance in reading. Based

(Text continues, page 35)

Figure 3.1   Passion Profiles Protocol

---

pas·sion (p²sh" . . . n) *n.* **1.** A powerful emotion, such as love, joy, hatred, or anger. **2.a.** Ardent love. **3.a.** Boundless enthusiasm . . .

Read the passion profiles, and identify the passion that most accurately describes who you are as an educator. If several fit (this will be true for many of you), choose the one that affects you the most or the one that seems most significant as you reflect on your practice over time (five minutes).

Without using the number of the passion profile, ask your colleagues questions, and find the people who chose the same profile you did (five minutes).

Directions for Small Groups:

1. Choose a facilitator or timer and a recorder or reporter.

2. Check to see if you all really share that passion. Then, talk about your school experiences together. What is it like to have this passion—to be this kind of educator? Each person in the group should have an opportunity to talk, uninterrupted, for two minutes (ten minutes).

3. Next, each person in the group privately identifies an actual student, by name, who has been affected by the group's profile. Write in your journal the following (five minutes):

   • What have I done with this student?

   • What's worked? What hasn't?

   • What else could I do?

   • What questions does this raise for me?

4. Talk as a group about the questions that teachers who share this passion are likely to have about their practice. List as many of these questions as you can (fifteen minutes).

   The recorder or reporter should write on the newsprint and should be ready to report out succinctly to the large group. Be sure to put your passion profile number at the top of the newsprint page.

5. Have the whole group debrief (after hearing from each passion profile group; fifteen minutes):

   • What strikes you as you listen to the passions of these educators? Listen for the silences. Where are they, and what do you make of them?

   • Which of the questions generated intrigues you the most? Why? How might you go about exploring this question with colleagues? What would you do first?

Figure 3.2   Passion Profiles

Passion 1: The Child

You became a teacher primarily because you wanted to make a difference in the life of a child. Perhaps you were one of those whose life was changed by a committed, caring teacher and you decided to become a teacher so that you could do that for other children. You are always curious about particular students whose work and/or behavior just don't seem to be in sync with the rest of the students in your class. You often wonder about how peer interactions seem to affect a student's likelihood to complete assignments, or what enabled one of your English language learner (ELL) students to make such remarkable progress seemingly overnight, or how to motivate a particular student to get into the habit of writing. You believe that understanding the unique qualities that each student brings to your class is the key to unlocking their full potential as learners.

Passion 2: The Curriculum

You are one of those teachers who are always "tinkering" with the curriculum in order to enrich the learning opportunities for you students. You have a thorough understanding of your content area. You attend conferences and subscribe to journals that help you to stay up on current trends affecting the curriculum that you teach. Although you are often dissatisfied with "what is" with respect to the prescribed curriculum in your school or district, you are almost always sure that you could do it better than the frameworks. You are always critiquing the existing curriculum and finding ways to make it better for the kids you teach—especially when you have a strong hunch that "there is a better way to do this."

Passion 3: Content Knowledge

You are at your best in the classroom when you have a thorough understanding of the content and/or topic you are teaching. Having to teach something you don't know much about makes you uncomfortable and always motivates you to hone up this area of your teaching knowledge base. You realize that what you know about what you are teaching will influence how you get it across to your students in a developmentally appropriate way. You spend a considerable amount of your personal time—both during the school year and in the summer—looking for books, material, workshops, and courses you can take that will strengthen your content knowledge.

Passion 4: Teaching Strategies

You are motivated most as a teacher by a desire to improve on and experiment with teaching strategies and techniques. You have experienced and understand the value of particular strategies to engage students in powerful learning and want to get really good at this stuff. Although you have become really comfortable with using cooperative learning with your students, there are many other

(Continued)

Figure 3.2 (Continued)

strategies and techniques that interest you and that you want to incorporate into your teaching repertoire.

Passion 5: The Relationship Between Beliefs and Professional Practice

You sense a "disconnect" between what you believe and what actually happens in your classroom and/or school. For example, you believe that a major purpose of schools is to produce citizens capable of contributing to and sustaining a democratic society, however, students in your class seldom get an opportunity to discuss controversial issues because you fear that the students you teach may not be ready and/or capable of this and you are concerned about losing control of the class.

Passion 6: The Intersection Between Your Personal and Professional Identities

You came into teaching from a previous career and often sense that your previous identity may be in conflict with your new identity as an educator. You feel ineffective and frustrated when your students or colleagues don't approach a particular task that is second nature to you because of your previous identity— writer, actor, artist, researcher, etc.—in the same way that you do. What keeps you up at night is how to use the knowledge, skills, and experiences you bring from your previous life to make powerful teaching and learning happen in your classroom and/or school.

Passion 7: Advocating Equity and Social Justice

You became an educator to change the world—to help create a more just, equitable, democratic, and peaceful planet. You are constantly thinking of ways to integrate issues of race, class, disability, power, etc., into your teaching; however, your global concerns for equity and social justice sometimes get in the way of your effectiveness as an educator—such as the backlash that resulted from the time you showed *Schindler's List* to your sixth-grade class, You know there are more developmentally appropriate ways to infuse difficult and complex issues into your teaching and want to learn more about how to do this with your students.

Passion 8: Context Matters

What keeps you up at night is how to keep students focused on learning despite the many disruptions that go on in your classroom or building on a daily basis. It seems that the school context conspires against everything that you know about teaching and learning: adults who don't model the behaviors they want to see reflected in the students; policies that are in conflict with the schools mission; and above all, a high-stakes testing environment that tends to restrain the kind of teaching and learning that you know really works for the students you teach.

on this analysis, the group developed a direction for their PLC work framed by this overarching question: What actions can we take as fourth-grade teachers to improve the reading achievement of our lowest-achieving students? To gain insights into this overarching question, members of this PLC framed three subquestions, each focused on a different action the PLC members would institute and study within their own classrooms.

One teacher instituted the strategy of repeated readings, an approach the PLC had read showed promise for students with learning disabilities and other students who struggled to learn to read well in the elementary school (Chard, Ketterlin-Geller, Baker, Doabler, & Apichatabutra, 2009), focusing the strategy of repeated readings specifically on the use of fractured fairy-tale plays. Fractured fairy-tale plays are humorous takes on traditional fairy-tales written in a script format for learners to read and perform. This teacher developed the following subquestion to guide her transfer of learning community work to date into her own classroom practice and subsequently contribute to the overarching question that framed the PLC work moving forward: What is the relationship between my fourth graders' fluency development and repeated readings of fractured fairy-tale plays?

A second teacher in this PLC instituted word walls, a literacy tool that consists of a collection of words systematically organized on a wall or bulletin board display that "grows" with students over time as they add to the wall based on different reading experiences they have in the classroom (Harmon, Wood, Hedrick, Vintinner, & Willeford, 2009). Word walls were being used successfully in first-grade classrooms in this school to foster phonemic awareness but not utilized by the fourth-grade teaching team. This teacher developed the following subquestion to guide her transfer of the learning community work into her own classroom practice to date and subsequently contribute to the overarching question that framed the PLC work moving forward: In what ways can word walls be effectively adopted for use with struggling readers in my fourth-grade class during literacy center time?

Finally, the third fourth-grade teacher on the team and the special education teacher were interested in exploring differentiation—another concept the PLC had been reading about as it related to reading instruction (Tomlinson, 2001). They decided to work together to institute the action of co-teaching, defined as a regular and a special education teacher planning lessons and teaching a subject together to a class of special and regular education students (Friend & Cook, 2000). These teachers developed the following subquestion to guide their transfer of the learning community work to date into their own practice and subsequently contribute to the overarching question that framed the PLC work moving forward: What role does co-teaching play in differentiating instruction during reading time for all learners in the class?

This learning community's guiding questions can be summarized as follows:

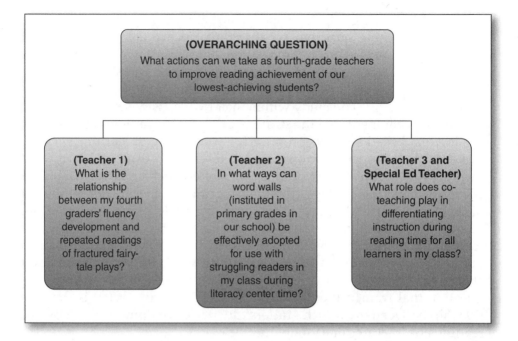

Each member of the PLC investigated his or her individual subquestions with support from the other PLC members who helped to plan the implementation of the strategy, observed PLC members as they were implementing the strategy, looked at data that were generated as the strategy was implemented to ascertain effectiveness, and subsequently implemented an adapted version of the strategy into their own classroom practice. At the end of the school year, all of the teachers were using repeated readings, word walls, and differentiation within their classrooms with the help or support of the special education teacher, who eventually engaged in co-teaching with all three fourth-grade teachers. The learning community was proud of the subsequent improvement in reading achievement of their lowest quartile students resulting from their collective investigation of the overarching question that had framed their PLC work that school year: What actions can we take as fourth-grade teachers to improve the reading achievement of our lowest-achieving students?

In sum, a single guiding question or an overarching question with multiple related subquestions can frame the work of a PLC. In addition, we have even observed PLCs function with all PLC members developing individual unrelated guiding questions for their work that emerge from their own personal passions about classroom practice. When this happens, the overarching guiding question of a PLC might be stated as, "In what ways can we, as teaching colleagues, support one another in the investigation of and improvement of our practice at our school?" Then, each PLC member individually crafts a personal question for exploration and investigation and PLC meeting time serves to support each individual PLC member as he or she explores his or her own personal question of practice.

Figure 3.3 Learning Community Matrix

Community Name: _____ Date Completed: _____			
K What do we **know** about this community?	**W** What do we **want** to know?	**P** What is our **plan** for finding out what we want to know?	**L** What have we **learned?** (This is to be completed after we analyze data.)

Whether your PLC establishes a direction through the development of one single question to explore together, one overarching collective question with related subquestions, or individual personal PLC member questions will depend upon what makes the most sense for the context within which your PLC work takes place as well as the preferences of the individual PLC members for how they wish to work together.

WHAT DOES ESTABLISHING A DIRECTION FOR YOUR PLC LOOK LIKE?

A guiding question sometimes develops naturally as a result of engagement in typical PLC meeting activity. More often, however, a PLC might dedicate one or more of its PLC meetings explicitly to the development of guiding question(s) to establish a long-term focus for the PLC work.

If PLC membership decides to investigate a collective question, the foci for the group's question and ideas for framing the question are brainstormed at this meeting. For example, a learning community matrix (Figure 3.3 on page 37) might be used to initiate dialogue around the formation of a collective question. In this activity, PLC members decide on a "name" for their community based on the work they have done to date. Next, the community completes the K box in their matrix by answering this question: What do we already **know** as a result of our PLC work to date? Then, members of the community complete the W box by answering this question: What do we **want** to know? Finally, members complete the third P box with a **plan** for finding out what they want to know. After this box is completed, the group works to translate the plan into the statement of a guiding question and tweak the question until all PLC members feel comfortable with the question and the direction for their shared work. At the end of a school year, the group returns to the matrix and completes the final L box stating what they have **learned** as a result of their collective work.

Similarly, if PLC membership decides to develop individual personal guiding questions, each member of the PLC might come to a meeting ready to share question(s) he or she is considering for exploration and investigation that school year. Sometimes PLC members journal prior to coming to this meeting or complete a reflective guide. Figures 3.4 and 3.5 at the end of this chapter share examples of a journaling prompt and a reflective guide that helped establish the direction of a PLC over time.

At the meeting itself, each individual takes a turn sharing a felt difficulty, dilemma, or tension in practice that has led to a question and then subsequently articulates his or her initial question. Dialogue about the dilemma and question can be guided by a protocol that helps each individual refine and further develop his or her guiding question:

FINE-TUNING A QUESTION FEEDBACK GROUP PROTOCOL

Developed by Nancy Fichtman Dana and Mickey MacDonald
Time frame: Fifteen minutes per PLC member

THINGS TO CONSIDER WHEN PROVIDING FEEDBACK:

- Is the question something your colleague is passionate about exploring?
- Is the question focused on student learning?
- Is the question focused on your colleague's own practice?
- Is the question a REAL question (a question whose answer is not known)?

Step 1: Framing and Sharing the Question (3–4 minutes)—The presenter shares the dilemma that led to his or her question and shares the question with the group.

Step 2: Probing Questions (6 minutes)—Participants pose probing questions about the dilemma and question. Probing questions are open-ended and designed to help the presenter think more deeply about the framing and articulation of his or her question as well as provide more information to the group about the presenter's thinking.

Sample Probing Questions:

- What is most important for you to learn related to your dilemma? In what ways does your question address what is important to you?
- In what ways might your students benefit from your exploration of this question?
- What do you already know about the topic of your dilemma? In what ways might gaining insights into your question enhance what you already know?
- What aspects of your dilemma are within your control? Outside your control? In what ways does your question reflect what you can control?

Step 3: Fine-Tuning the Question (4–5 minutes)—Based on what they heard in Steps 1 and 2, participants provide suggestions for fine-tuning the wording of or reframing the question.

TIP: *Questions are generally not phrased in a dichotomous (yes/no) fashion. If a question is phrased dichotomously, try rewording using the following question starters:*

- In what ways does _____?

- What is the relationship between _____?

(Continued)

(Continued)

- How do students experience _____?
- What happens when _____?
- How does _____?

Step 4: Presenter Thanks (1 minute maximum)—The presenter briefly shares insights he or she gained into his or her question and thanks group members for their support.

Indira Gandhi once said, "The power to question is the basis of all human progress." For the work of your PLC to progress over time, establish a direction for your work together using the power to question collectively and/or individually as a guide.

Questions for Discussion

1. Under what conditions do you believe each of the following formations of guiding questions would work best to provide direction for the work of a PLC?

   - One common PLC question all members explore together
   - One overarching PLC guiding question with related subquestions explored by individuals or subsets of individuals within the PLC
   - Individualized, personal questions developed by each PLC member

2. This chapter introduced and described a number of different PLC activities and protocols to use for different purposes when developing a direction for PLC work (i.e., I-MAP, passion profile, learning community matrix, journaling, reflective guide, fine-tuning a question feedback group protocol).

   - Which one of these activities or protocols would you feel most comfortable using yourself and why?
   - How and when could you use this activity or protocol in your own PLC work?
   - Which of these activities or protocols would you feel least comfortable using yourself and why?

- • When and why might you use this activity or protocol in your own PLC work, and what, if anything, might help you become more comfortable with its use?

3. What are some questions you might wish to explore within an existing PLC you currently have membership in or a PLC you might become a member of in the future?

Figure 3.4   Journaling Prompt

Think of the work you have done with your students this year.

What did not meet the expectations you had?

Was it "good" but could have been better?

What would benefit from being looked at with colleagues?

What would you have brought to be tuned with a colleague?

What would you have brought to be tuned with a protocol?

Describe the work, and come up with a focus question that you might use.

Figure 3.5   Reflective Guide

**LEARNING FROM EXAMINATION
OF STUDENT OR PROFESSIONAL WORK**

In preparation for our January meeting, please use this guide to do the following:

- Identify a question about your practice.
- Select student or professional work that relates most directly to your question.

1. What questions do I have about my practice as an educator?

2. Which of these questions (from #1) most directly affect student learning? Why?

3. Of the questions generated in #2, which ONE question do I have a passion to learn more about with the help of other colleagues, and do I think most directly affects student learning? (This is my inquiry question.)

4. What student or professional work do I have that relates most directly to this question? How does this work relate to my question?

Please bring at least six copies of the work you have identified along with this completed sheet to the January meeting.

4

Developing a PLC Action Learning Plan

WHAT A PLC ACTION LEARNING PLAN IS AND WHY IT'S IMPORTANT

With a professional learning community (PLC) direction established and captured by guiding question(s), the next step is developing an action plan to address the question(s). The following short vignette demonstrates the importance of devoting time to creating a plan for how the work of your PLC will unfold:

> *An aging man had lived his entire life in the same small town. Approaching his sixtieth birthday, he decided to venture out of his small town to explore the ways people lived in other parts of the world. Excited by the prospect of his journey, he filled his car up with gas and began driving. He had some general notions of where he might head but did not bother to chart a course for his travels or bring a road map. Before long, he found himself wandering aimlessly from road to road, town to town, and he had lost sight of why he began this trip in the first place. He returned to the comfort of his home without the enrichment or insights that travel can bring.*

Like the man in the scenario, in the absence of a well-developed plan for the work of a PLC, the group risks making little or no progress in their learning, getting lost, and even returning to the comfort of the ways their teaching has always been done without the benefits and insights that PLC work can bring. Hence, it is important to devote some PLC time to constructing a road map and charting a course for the learning you wish to accomplish together over time rather than progressing somewhat aimlessly from one PLC meeting to the next.

A PLC work plan usually includes a statement of the guiding question(s) of the PLC to remind the PLC of its general direction and focus as well as a projected timeline for desired PLC activities that will help the group gain insights into their guiding question(s). Over time, PLC activities generally include but are not limited to the following:

- Selection and reading of high-quality literature related to the topic of your PLC work
- Articulation of curriculum and/or teaching actions PLC members develop and try together related to their question(s)
- Ways in which the PLC will collect and analyze *multiple* types of data (i.e., student work, observations, videos, digital pictures, surveys, reflective journals, progress monitoring tools, grades, standardized assessment measure scores) to understand and document the ways PLC members' actions are contributing to student learning
- Ways the PLC will share its learning with other educators within and/or outside of the school

HOW TO DEVELOP A
PLC ACTION LEARNING PLAN

Whether your PLC has elected to explore a single question together; one overarching PLC guiding question with related subquestions explored by individuals or subsets of individuals within the PLC; or individualized, personal questions developed by each PLC member, the process of developing a PLC action learning plan can be accomplished by dedicating one PLC meeting to this purpose. In the situation where a PLC has selected to explore one single PLC guiding question or overarching question, one member of the PLC may be designated to begin this meeting by stating and posting the agreed-upon PLC question and facilitate conversation among PLC members that will result in devising a plan to systematically explore that question. Facilitating PLC conversation that will result in the development of an action plan generally includes discussion of questions such as the following:

- What knowledge is important for us to critically consume through readings and other sources to help us gain insights into our question?
- What teaching actions might we take to address our question?
- How will we collect data to gain insights into our actions?
- When will we collect the data?

- Who will collect the data?
- How will we analyze this data?
- How will we share the results of our work with others?

As these questions are addressed, the designated meeting facilitator (or any other group member) takes notes on chart paper and subsequently translates these notes into an organized plan for the group as the PLC meeting comes to a close.

In the situation where a PLC has selected individualized, personal questions developed by each PLC member, it is often helpful for each individual to come to the PLC planning meeting with a brief, one- to two-page individual action plan already developed, and enough copies for each member of the group. Hence, rather than the PLC planning meeting *ending* with one plan that is constructed at the same time by the entire group, the PLC planning meeting *begins* with an individual PLC member presenting his or her already developed plan and receiving feedback from PLC members to fine-tune that plan. Subsequently, each member of the PLC takes a turn presenting and receiving feedback on his or her individual plan. When all members of the PLC have received feedback, the meeting ends with the writing of reflective statements on the planning experience.

Figure 4.1 (pages 46–47) provides one example of what a one- to two-page individual PLC member's learning plan might look like. In addition, Figure 4.2 (found on page 48) provides an example of a protocol that can be used to structure a PLC planning meeting when each individual member of a PLC is developing an individualized action plan. We have found that it is helpful to use a protocol to provide structure to PLC action planning meetings focused on individuals sharing their own learning plans with the group to be sure everyone gets equal time for feedback. If your PLC has more than five members, we suggest you break into two groups of three or four to engage with this protocol at your PLC action planning meeting.

WHAT MIGHT DEVELOPING
AN ACTION LEARNING PLAN LOOK LIKE?

We illustrate what developing an action learning plan might look like based upon the PLC work of our good friend and colleague, Kevin Berry. We have observed Kevin both participating in and facilitating PLC meetings for years. In the scenario that follows, Kevin was asked by his PLC to serve as the facilitator for their next meeting that would be devoted to the group developing their action learning plan for the upcoming school year.

Kevin's PLC had been meeting since just before school opened in August. During the group's early meetings, they engaged in a series of conversations about their struggling students' needs and a series of

Figure 4.1   PLC Action Learning Plan: Independent Reading

Helena Fishbein

Purpose:

My eleventh-grade Intensive Reading and English III classes are composed entirely of students who struggle with reading comprehension and were placed in this class based on failing scores on the tenth-grade state reading assessment. Based on research of effective methods for helping striving readers, I decided to require twenty minutes of independent reading in class from a book of the student's own choosing, three days a week in class, and three nights for homework (a total of two hours a week). I tried to keep accountability minimal and useful so students are required to keep a reading log, where they summarize in three sentences what they read in the past twenty minutes. In the past, I have had mixed feelings about independent reading in class because of behavior issues and assumed ineffectiveness. The research convinced me that independent reading is valuable and engaging to students. It also reminded me that part of my goal as an English teacher is to create lifelong readers—not just students who can pass a standardized test. So what I want to know is if, as the research states, independent reading is a valuable component of my curriculum. Is it working?

Question:

How does emphasizing independent reading in an eleventh-grade intensive reading class influence low-achieving students' fluency, comprehension, and perception of self as a reader?

Subquestions:

- How does allowing time for independent reading influence attitudes toward reading in general?
- How do students react to "forced" independent reading?
- To what extent do students enjoy what they are reading?
- How often do these students read without being required to read?

Teaching Action:

Students already read in class Tuesdays, Wednesdays, and Thursdays for twenty minutes, with an extra five minutes to write a three-sentence summary in their reading log. Their required homework is to read an additional twenty minutes at home on Tuesdays, Wednesdays, and Thursdays and then to write a summary. I plan to continue with this routine next quarter and focus on my students who scored a Level 1 on last year's reading state assessment. I will follow three students from periods 2 and 3, six students from periods 4 and 5, and two students from periods 6 and 7. Of these, seven are Exceptional Student Education (ESE), and four are general education. I plan to conduct observations while reading occurs in class, interviews about reading at random times throughout the week that I will later record, surveys, anecdotal data, and fluency probes, as well as looking for increases in reading comprehension scores on class assessments.

Actions and Data Collection:

- Research on independent reading in high school lower-level reading classes
- Scores on various state assessments
- Fluency probes
- Surveys
- Observations
- Approximate number of words read per week at a given Lexile level
- Interviews
- Reading logs

Timeline:

- October

  o Create a spreadsheet with scores of students that I want to follow:

    o FCAT reading score from Spring 2012
    o Baseline test score
    o FAIR reading comprehension scores (Spring 2012 and Fall 2012)
    o Past ACT reading comprehension assessment scores

  o Read research on independent reading.

- November and December

  o Administer reading survey.
  o Administer fluency probe.
  o Observe students while independently reading, and record notes.
  o Interview students about what they are reading and if they are enjoying it.
  o Collect and photocopy reading logs.
  o Record the approximate number of words read this week and Lexile level.
  o Record ACT reading assessment results.

- January

  o Bring collected student data to the PLC meeting, and receive feedback from the group using the "looking at student work" protocol.
  o Chart next steps based on what is learned at this PLC meeting.

readings related to engaged instruction. One of the topics that generated much attention from these early group discussions was the role that culturally responsive teaching might play in helping the teachers reach their struggling students. The group had learned that culturally responsive teaching uses the cultural knowledge, prior experiences, and performance styles of diverse students to make learning more appropriate and effective by teaching to and through the strengths of these students (Gay, 2000). Additionally, the group had come to recognize culturally responsive teaching as multidimensional, including elements of curriculum content, learning context, classroom climate, student–teacher relationships, instructional techniques, and performance assessments. As a result

Figure 4.2   PLC Individual Action Plan Discussion Protocol

Suggested Group Size: Three to four

Suggested Time Frame: Fifteen minutes per group member

1. Select a timekeeper.

2. The presenter hands out a hard copy of the learning plan to each member of the group.

3. Group members *silently* read the plan, making notes of issues or questions they might like to raise in discussion with the presenter (four minutes). As group members read the plan, the presenter engages in a writing activity to complete the following sentences:

Something I would like help with on my learning plan is _____.

One thing this group needs to know about me to better prepare them to assist me is _____.

4. At the end of four minutes (or when it is clear that every member of the group has completed reading and taking notes on the action plan and the presenter has finished his or her response to the writing activity), the timekeeper invites the presenter to read his or her sentence completion activity out loud (no more than one minute).

5. Participants talk to each other as if the presenter were not in the room while the presenter remains silent and takes notes (approximately ten minutes). Participants focus on *each* of the following:

   • Provide "warm feedback" on the plan. This is feedback that is positive in nature and identifies areas of strength (one to two minutes).

   • Address the area the presenter would like help on.

6. The timekeeper asks the presenter to summarize the key points made during discussion that he or she wishes to consider in refining his or her action plan (one minute).

---

of this shared learning and identification of a shared goal, the group developed the following questions to provide direction for their PLC:

• How do we create more culturally responsive teaching in our classrooms?

• What happens to student learning when we create more culturally responsive teaching?

This work would be important as it connected to a larger context including both their school's improvement plan, their district's initiative, and their community's needs.

In mid-October, the group met to develop their action learning plan, asking Kevin to serve as the facilitator of this particular meeting. They began this meeting by devoting ten minutes to a protocol called "Connections," developed by Gene Thompson-Grove and designed to help learning community members build a bridge from where they are or have been (mentally, physically, etc.) to where they will be going and what they will be doing in this PLC meeting (see the School Reform Initiative [SRI] website for additional instructions on this protocol: http://schoolre forminitiative.org/doc/connections.pdf).

Once "Connections" was completed, Kevin began, "We left our last PLC meeting with two questions that we agreed to explore together this year." Kevin pointed to the chart paper he had hung up prior to the start of the meeting that read, "How do we create more culturally responsive teaching in our classrooms? What happens to student learning when we create more culturally responsive teaching?" He knew it would be important to have these questions front and center during this meeting in order to keep the group's eye on the goal.

He continued, "At today's meeting, we agreed to develop a plan to address these questions, but first I need to confirm that we are all comfortable with the decision to pursue these questions. The floor is open for thoughts and comments for five minutes."

PLC membership dialogue ensued, reaffirming the membership's commitment toward culturally responsive practices.

At the end of five minutes, Kevin spoke, "I hear we all share a passion and commitment to devote our PLC work to the exploration of these questions, so let's begin by discussing what we need to gain insights into these questions. Let's brainstorm a list of the information we would need to help us answer the questions and then match up actions we can take in our classrooms and data collection strategies that would help us generate this information. This is a time to be open to all possibilities and not limit our brainstorming in any way, so let's begin."

Kevin drew a two-column chart on the whiteboard that he filled in as PLC members generated ideas. The group began by generating a list of the types of information that they believed would help them better understand their children and their children's culture and Kevin listed this information in the left-hand column.

When no new ideas were forthcoming from PLC group members, Kevin stood and admired the chart they were creating together. They had created a lengthy list of areas they knew they needed more knowledge about in order to teach these struggling students. Next, Kevin brainstormed with the group and scripted the ideas of the kinds of actions and data that would help them get the information they deemed potentially useful. As a result, the group generated the following chart:

PLC Guiding Questions: How do we create more culturally responsive teaching in our classrooms? What happens to student learning when we create more culturally responsive teaching?	
Information That Would Help Us Answer Our Questions	*Actions and Data Collection Strategies That Would Generate This Information*
Find out more about the neighborhoods our students live in.	Conduct neighborhood and/or home visitations, and take notes.
Find out what parents expect from the school community.	Survey parents. Conduct home visits, and talk to parents.
Find out how our students are performing in each academic area and sub-area.	Assess data.
Find out what goals students set for themselves.	Conduct student interviews or surveys.
Find out what management patterns are familiar to students. Find out what teachers expect from their students and how they encourage students to meet expectations and recognize their accomplishments.	Have focus group interviews with teachers. Conduct classroom observations.
Get to know students' learning style preferences.	Conduct a survey.
Utilize content and resources that connect to students' backgrounds.	Do a search for books, articles, and Web resources. Journal about new strategies that might benefit our students and why.
Develop a variety of learning activities that are engaging and reflective of students' backgrounds (cooperative learning, literature circles, community projects).	Do a search for books, articles, and Web resources. Journal about new strategies that might benefit our students and why.
Find out how students respond (both learning and engagement) to various teaching strategies.	Analyze student work. Observe. Distribute student feedback sheets. Journal about changes we are seeing in our teaching and with our students.

Although the group seemed pleased with their list, some of them looked overwhelmed at the amount of work that might follow. As a result, Kevin proceeded to ask the group to carefully evaluate their chart as he posed the following questions:

- What aspects of the chart we generated together surprised you?
- What aspects of the chart we generated together would be great actions to take and sources of data to gain but impractical to do?
- What actions and sources of data do you think would be most valuable and why?
- What structures need to be in place to support our effort?

Through discussion of these questions, the group committed to some specific actions to include in their PLC learning plan. For example, at the beginning of their work together, the group members decided to distribute a survey to both parents and students to better understand their own goals as well as expectations they had of the school. During the bulk of the year, the group also believed that saving student work samples, tracking student growth on assessments, as well as notes from peer observations would help them make sense of their ability to transfer new ideas about culturally responsive teaching to the classroom. Each of the members also committed to keeping a journal that included observation notes as well as personal reflections on his or her teaching. Finally, they decided that by asking students to complete feedback sheets after engaging in culturally relevant teaching, they would learn a great deal.

Kevin continued, "Okay, great, we have a plan! Now, we need to establish when and how we are going to do this plan. Our PLC meetings are the first Wednesday of every month. How about if I list our monthly meeting dates on the board, and we can use that to set goals for when and how we will accomplish what we agreed upon."

Through discussion, the following timeline emerged:

How do we create more culturally responsive teaching in our classrooms? What happens to student learning when we create more culturally responsive teaching?		
Month	*Before Meeting*	*During Meeting*
September	• Read articles on culturally responsive teaching (all members).	• "Connections." • Have a text-based discussion on articles.

(Continued)

(Continued)

Month	Before Meeting	During Meeting
	• Review your own student assessment data.	• Establish groups' shared goals and inquiry questions. • Reflect.
October	• Develop, distribute, and collect parent and student surveys (Jane, Mark, and Beth). • Collect and review baseline assessment data (each classroom teacher). • Visit neighborhoods (entire PLC; invite pastor).	• "Connections." • Analyze parent and student surveys. • Engage in a text-based discussion of culturally responsive teaching strategies. • Reflect.
November	• Conduct student interviews (each teacher completes three interviews). • Have peer observations (each teacher observes one other group member). • Collect student work as the teacher implements culturally responsive teaching strategies (each teacher). • Take field notes as each teacher implements culturally responsive teaching strategies.	• "Connections." • Use tuning protocols or dilemma protocols focused on teachers sharing their efforts to engage in culturally responsive teaching strategies (three presenters; four groups). • Analyze student interviews. • Reflect.
December	• Read the article about culturally responsive teaching strategies (each teacher). • Have peer observations (each teacher observes one other group member). • Collect student work. • Take field notes as each teacher implements culturally responsive teaching strategies.	• "Connections." • Engage in a text-based discussion of culturally responsive teaching strategies. • Use tuning protocols or dilemma protocols focused on teachers sharing their efforts to engage in culturally responsive teaching strategies (three presenters; four groups).

Month	Before Meeting	During Meeting
	• Review student assessment data (each teacher).	• Reflect.
January	• Collect student work. • Have peer observations (each teacher observes one other group member). • Take field notes as each teacher implements culturally responsive teaching strategies.	• "Connections." • Use protocols to analyze student work. • Use consultancy to explore dilemmas you are having with your students. • Reflect.
February	• Collect student work. • Have peer observations (each teacher observes one other group member). • Take field notes as each teacher implements culturally responsive teaching strategies.	• "Connections." • Use protocols to analyze student work. • Use consultancy to explore dilemmas you are having with your students. • Reflect.
March	• Collect student work samples. • Take field notes as each teacher implements culturally responsive teaching strategies. • Review student assessment data (each teacher). • Meet with Kevin (each teacher met with Kevin or another trained coach in the school to closely examine the individual data that they had collected).	• "Connections." • Use protocols to analyze student work. • Use consultancy to explore dilemmas you are having with your students. • Reflect.
April	• Repeat survey. • Repeat the subset of student interviews. • Gather all data. • Engage in preliminary analysis by reading through own data.	• "Connections." • Analyze survey data. • Analyze data across learning community meetings to generate overarching findings from the year's inquiry work. • Reflect.

(Continued)

(Continued)

Month	Before Meeting	During Meeting
May	• Develop the presentation.	• Provide an overview of results to the principal. • Share at faculty meeting and with district office. • Reflect.

As shown, this plan integrated many of the protocols for looking at student work, resolving dilemmas, and generating lesson plans that are offered by the SRI as tools for deepening teaching practice. Additionally, the plan required the learning community members to do some work outside of the learning community meeting times. The school principal was able to allocate this important time for the teachers and Kevin to engage in the professional work associated with membership in a PLC.

Kevin volunteered to type up their plan and ended the PLC meeting with a reminder: "We have engaged in some hard work today to develop a plan for our PLC work. I'll type up our work and e-mail it to everyone before our next meeting. I would also like to volunteer to keep a notebook of the artifacts we generate from our PLC meetings together, but I think we should each keep our own PLC notebook as well. Just as I will document our collective work, I think it makes sense for each of us to document our individual work toward making sense of how culturally responsive teaching is working for us and our students.

"I think it's also important to keep in mind that even though we developed a plan for our PLC work, it's okay for us to deviate from our plan as our work unfolds. We may discover something along the way that leads us in a new direction. We can help each other remain open to shifts in our work along the way by periodically returning to this plan and suggesting modifications. We need to remember that the plan we constructed today is important to provide direction, but it isn't set in stone! Let's spend our last five minutes writing a reflection on today's meeting."

PLC group members took out a piece of paper and jotted down their feelings and thoughts about the ways their PLC planning meeting had transpired.

Questions for Discussion

1. What do you believe to be the value of dedicating one PLC meeting to the development of an action learning plan?

2. What do you believe might be challenging about dedicating one PLC meeting to the development of an action learning plan?

3. Two different approaches to dedicating one meeting of a PLC to the development of an action learning plan were illustrated in this chapter:

    - In the situation where a PLC has selected to explore one single PLC guiding question or overarching question, one member of the PLC facilitates conversation among PLC members that will result in devising a collective plan to systematically explore the PLC question at the end of the meeting.
    - In the situation where a PLC has selected individualized, personal questions developed by each PLC member, PLC members bring individual action plans to the meeting, and the meeting consists of each member taking a turn sharing and receiving feedback on his or her individual plan.

Compare and contrast these two meeting approaches. What are the benefits and drawbacks of each meeting type?

4. Kevin's PLC began each of their meetings with a protocol called "Connections" developed by Gene Thompson-Grove. Review this protocol at http://schoolreforminitiative.org/doc/connections.pdf.

    What are some reasons Kevin's PLC elected to use this protocol to begin each one of their PLC meetings? Would you select this protocol to use at the start of your own PLC meetings? Why or why not? What are some other ways you might begin a PLC meeting in order to help members "connect" with one another?

5. In the plan that Kevin's PLC developed, they noted they would use various protocols for different purposes throughout the year as their PLC work unfolded. Visit the SRI website to explore different protocols that Kevin's PLC might use for different purposes (www.school reforminitiative.org/protocols).

    - If you were a member of Kevin's PLC, which of these specific protocols might you find useful for your work at different times in the year?
    - When and why might you use any of these protocols in your own PLC work?

5

Analyzing Data in Your PLC

WHAT DATA ANALYSIS IS AND WHY IT'S IMPORTANT

As you work through your professional learning community (PLC) action learning plan, your PLC will collect and generate lots of data. For these data to become meaningful, your PLC will work together to analyze the data that emerge throughout your work together. Data analysis is an ongoing and critical component of PLC work and can be defined simply as developing an understanding of what your data are telling you based on a close, careful, and critical examination of them over time.

The process of data analysis is twofold: formative and summative. Formative data analysis takes place throughout the work of your PLC. The processes of data collection and data analysis do not exist independently of one another and proceed in a chronological lockstep manner. Rather, these processes are iterative in nature. As PLCs analyze data, they seek to understand what those data mean drawing on the diverse perspectives of group members. The members use these understandings to make decisions about instruction and determine the next steps in their PLC work.

Several protocols exist to help PLCs in the formative data analysis process. These protocols include the "ATLAS—Looking at Data" protocol, the

"Data Driven Dialogue" protocol, and "Data Mining Protocol." We suggest reviewing these protocols on the School Reform Initiative (SRI) website (www.schoolreforminitiative.org/protocols) to better understand the ways PLC conversation about data can be structured in systematic and intentional ways.

While important insights are gleaned from the process of formative data analysis just described, as one nears the end of a PLC action learning plan, it's critical to engage in summative data analysis as well. Summative data analysis involves the group members stepping back at the end of the implementation of the PLC action learning plan. The individuals take a look at the entire data set generated from the PLC work as a whole. This step is often completed in preparation for discussing the PLC's work with other members. As members representing diverse perspectives review and discuss the data, new and different types of insights are gleaned. After sharing these insights, the group member collaboratively engages in summative discussion that results in insights that cannot be gleaned from independent looks at isolated portions of data that was completed during the formative data analysis efforts.

HOW TO ANALYZE DATA

If members of a PLC have selected to explore one single PLC guiding question or overarching question, the PLC will have a number of meetings that occur after the action learning plan meeting during which time the PLC will look at data collected at different points in their work along the way. After a series of these meetings where the PLC has looked closely at individual sets of data, the PLC will reach a point where it is nearing the end of data collection as it is articulated in the PLC's action learning plan. At this time, it is a good idea to dedicate one entire meeting (often for an extended time period) to the summative data analysis process.

For example, let's return to Kevin's PLC introduced in Chapter 4 and their focus on creating more culturally responsive teaching for the students in their school. Early in their PLC work, they administered a survey to all of the teachers in their building to capture their thoughts about culturally responsive teaching as well as their students' needs. At one of the PLC meetings, a protocol called "Chalk Talk" was used to facilitate the discussion of the survey data as a part of this PLC's formative data analysis.

The first ten minutes of the meeting was devoted to each PLC member reading through the typed-up responses to the surveys. Next, Kevin, the meeting facilitator, briefly explained that his PLC was going to engage in a "Chalk Talk" (http://schoolreforminitiative.org/doc/chalk_talk.pdf) to generate ideas about the survey responses. This was a silent activity—no one was to talk and anyone could add to the "Chalk Talk" as they pleased by commenting on other people's ideas simply by drawing a connecting line to the comment. In essence, rather than engaging in conversation with spoken words, they were to engage in conversation with words written on paper. Next, Kevin hung up a large roll of chart paper and gave everyone in the group a marker. He wrote the following question in a big circle in the center of the chart paper: What did you learn from reading the survey responses? For fifteen minutes, individuals silently took turns writing on the chart paper about responses that surprised them, responses that confirmed their dissatisfaction with the current state of inclusive practices in their building, and responses that gave direction for their future. Kevin took a picture of the "Chalk Talk" with his phone to document this discussion and to create the ability for the PLC to return to the conversation later in their work together if desired. Over the next few months, Kevin's PLC continued to collect data to inform their guiding questions according to their plan, discussing these data at PLC meetings in various ways.

As they were approaching the last third of the school year, PLC membership was nearing the end of all they had planned to do together, and it was time to look at their work as a whole. This was accomplished by dedicating one PLC meeting to this purpose. Two weeks prior to the date set for that meeting, Kevin, who had kept the PLC notebook throughout the year with all documents produced at their meetings, made enough copies of all of the data collected for each member of the PLC, placing each different copy in its own notebook. Kevin gave one notebook to each PLC member and requested that they read through the entire notebook once in preparation for their summative data analysis meeting. He also asked them to read through anything they had collected personally about their own use of culturally responsive teaching that they had been saving in their own personal PLC notebooks.

Together, at this extended two-hour data analysis meeting, the PLC used a four-step process to analyze the contents of their notebooks: description, sensemaking, interpretation, and implications. In the description phase, PLC members spent fifteen minutes simply describing their data as a whole. This was accomplished by each member of the PLC taking a turn in round-robin fashion simply sharing something they noticed in the data as they had read through it in their notebooks to prepare for this meeting. As each PLC member shared, one member of the PLC noted each contribution on chart paper for all to see as the group continued to closely, carefully, and critically examine all they had done during their year of work together. Rounds continued until no member of the group had anything left to contribute to their growing data description chart.

During the next thirty-minute segment of the meeting, the group pondered the chart they had created together and began a sensemaking process by engaging in a group exercise using sticky notes to create a visual representation of the PLC thinking in relationship to the data they had just described. Each PLC member placed a different colored small sticky note next to the entry listed on the chart that corresponded to these statements:

- This point on our chart is most important to me personally (yellow sticky note).
- This point on the chart is most important to our school (pink sticky note).
- This point on the chart stands out from the rest (green sticky note).
- This point on the chart needs further clarification and/or investigation (blue sticky note).

The group discussed where different colored sticky notes had clustered as well as lone sticky notes and what this meant to the ways they were making sense of the data as a group. They used this discussion as an impetus to organize their data to discuss claims they could make about what they had learned from their PLC work that school year, moving to the next segment of their meeting focused on interpretation. At this time, the group spent about forty-five minutes giving voice to what they had learned collectively in their PLC work and what that learning might mean to each individual within the PLC as well as the PLC as a whole.

As a final step to this meeting, the group turned the discussion to implications of their work together that school year. To facilitate this discussion, they once again returned to the use of the "Chalk Talk" protocol they had used earlier in their work together to analyze responses to a survey the group had conducted at the start of their work. This time, three questions guided their discussion:

- What have we learned about culturally responsive teaching?
- What are the implications of our learning?
- What changes might we suggest for our practice based on what we learned?

The group ended their meeting by using their chalk talk to plan a short presentation about their PLC work to be delivered to the principal and the rest of the faculty next month.

Kevin's PLC data analysis meeting depicts how working with colleagues to analyze data might be accomplished when a PLC is exploring one single PLC guiding question or overarching question together. In the situation where a PLC is exploring individualized, personal questions developed by each PLC member, we have found it is helpful to structure summative data analysis meetings as sharing and feedback sessions, where each member of the PLC comes to a meeting ready to share what he or she is learning from a close, careful, and critical look at his or her data conducted individually prior to the meeting. During the data analysis meeting, individuals present to the group what they are learning from their data so far. We have developed a protocol (Figure 5.1) to focus each individual and to be sure that everyone in the group gets equal time for sharing and feedback. If your PLC has more than five members, we suggest you break into two groups of three or four to engage with this protocol, or hold two separate data analysis feedback meetings with half of your group presenting during the first meeting and the other half presenting at the second. We have found

Figure 5.1   Data Analysis Protocol

Helping Your Colleagues Make Sense of What They Learned

Suggested Group Size: Four

Suggested Time Frame: Twenty-five to thirty minutes per group member

Step 1: Presenter Shares His or Her PLC Exploration (four minutes)

Presenter briefly shares with his or her group members the focus or purpose of his or her PLC work, what his or her guiding question(s) were, how data were collected, and the initial sense that the presenter has made of his or her data. Completing the following sentences prior to discussion may help presenter organize his or her thoughts prior to sharing:

- The issue, dilemma, problem, or interest that led me to this exploration of teaching was _____.

- Therefore, the purpose of my work was to _____.

- My guiding question(s) was _____.

- I collected data by _____.

- So far, three discoveries I've made from reading through my data are as follows:_____.

Step 2: Group Members Ask Clarifying Questions (three minutes)

Group members ask questions that have factual answers to clarify their understanding of the inquiry, such as, How many students did you work with?

Step 3: Group Members Ask Probing Questions (seven to ten minutes)

The group then asks probing questions of the presenter. These questions are worded so that they help the presenter clarify and expand his or her thinking about what he or she is learning from the data. During this ten-minute time frame, the presenter may respond to the group's questions, **but there is no discussion by the**

(Continued)

Figure 5.1 (Continued)

---

group of the presenter's responses. Every member of the group should pose at least one question of the presenter.

Step 4: Group Members Discuss the Data Analysis (six minutes)

The group talks with each other about the data analysis presented, discussing such questions as follows: What did we hear? What didn't we hear that we think might be relevant? What assumptions seem to be operating? Does any data not seem to fit with the presenter's analysis? What might be some additional ways to look at the presenter's data? During this discussion, members of the group work to deepen the data analysis. **The presenter doesn't speak during this discussion but instead listens and takes notes.**

Step 5: Presenter Reflection (three minutes)

The presenter reflects on what he or she heard and what he or she is now thinking, sharing with the group anything that particularly resonated for him or her during any part of the group members' data analysis discussion.

Step 6: Reflection on the Process (two minutes)

The group shares thoughts about how the discussion worked for the group.

---

that it is also helpful to have presenting individuals spend about five minutes completing a sentence completion activity (Figure 5.2) prior to beginning the protocol to help them organize their thoughts.

WHAT MIGHT ANALYZING DATA LOOK LIKE?

To provide contrast to the work of Kevin's PLC described previously, we illustrate what a data analysis meeting might look like for a PLC where each member was pursuing an individual question throughout the year. To do so, we introduce a reader's theater script to illustrate the use of the data analysis protocol presented in this chapter. This script can be read individually, or you may wish to read this together in your PLC by assigning "parts" in an effort for your PLC to "feel" what it is like to engage in deep discussion with one another using a protocol.

The five-member high school PLC depicted in this reader's theater was coached by a teacher, Leanne, who had participated in SRI training as part of her district's focus on learning community work. The script depicts the story of Chris, an English teacher, and the ways the data analysis protocol worked to help him think about the data he had collected to date in the exploration of his own personal guiding question.

Figure 5.2   Sentence Completion Activity

The issue, dilemma, problem, or interest that led me to this exploration of teaching was _____

_____

_____

_____.

Therefore, the purpose of my work was to _____

_____

_____

_____.

My guiding question(s) was _____

_____

_____

_____.

I collected data by _____

_____

_____

_____.

So far, three discoveries I've made from reading through my data are as follows:

1. _____

_____

_____

_____

2. _____

_____

_____

_____

3. _____

_____

_____

_____

THE STORY OF CHRIS, A PLC, AND A DATA ANALYSIS PROTOCOL

Characters:

- Narrator
- Leanne, the coach of the learning community
- Chris, an English teacher presenting the data from his work to members of his PLC
- Mickey, a teacher in the learning community
- Joan, a teacher in the learning community
- Sherri, a teacher in the learning community

Narrator: Over the past several years, Chris had developed a passion for technology. As an early adopter, he was one of the first to own his own tablet, have the latest smartphone, develop his own website, and tweet at his school. As he both enjoyed and benefited from the personal use of technology, through the years, he slowly introduced a number of technological advances into his instruction of American literature for high school juniors. He believed that the meaningful integration of technology into his instruction held promise for adding variety to the traditional literature discussions he held in the classroom and enriching students' understandings of the great American novels they covered in eleventh grade.

Chris was in his first year as a member of a PLC at his school. Chris became a member of this group at the suggestion of his principal and found membership in this group to be a painless way to earn the professional development points required by the state to renew his teaching license. Unlike previous professional development "sit and get" workshops, he actually was enjoying the PLC experience and the support he was receiving from other teachers as he explored an individual question about his practice focused on his technology passion. Supported by the members of his PLC, Chris was exploring the use of Weblogs with his honors/AP students to discuss the novel *Moby Dick*.

To gain insights into the ways blogging might enhance in-class discussions, Chris created an action learning plan that included setting up a site, reviewing students' posts, and developing a questionnaire students completed focused on their perceptions of the blogging experience. Chris also saved all of his lesson plans and in-class work students completed throughout the *Moby Dick* unit. Chris developed a series of "blog prompts" to initiate the students' participation on the site and sometimes assigned responding to the prompt as homework.

He had been working on his action learning plan for some time, and early in his attempt to introduce blogging into his unit on *Moby Dick*, had brought some samples of student work to his PLC meeting to review together. Since that time, however, other members of his PLC had been bringing student work related to their personal questions to the PLC, and it had been some time since Chris had received feedback from his colleagues on his own work. At the last meeting, Leanne suggested they devote their next meeting to helping each other begin the process of summative data analysis as they would soon be entering the final nine-week marking period, indicating the end of the school year and the PLC work together would soon be coming to a close. To prepare for this meeting, Chris was to read through all of the data he had collected so far and complete a sheet of open-ended statements to bring to their next meeting (Figure 5.2).

Leanne began this meeting by encouraging everyone to take one of her famous brownies she had brought to share. She then handed out the data analysis protocol (Figure 5.1) and reviewed the protocol procedures with the group. She then began the meeting.

Leanne: I know many of you are at a point where you've collected a ton of data, and while we each have been bringing small samples of student work and other data to our PLC meetings over time to receive formative feedback, I think it's time to turn our gaze to looking at the data you have been collecting throughout our PLC work as a whole. I think this exercise could really help each of you clarify what your data might be telling you and where you might go next. Who would like to present first?

Narrator: Chris volunteered.

Chris: I'll go, although I'm not sure you all can help me too much. You see, I feel like I'm not really learning anything from my data. This whole blog experience I set out to do isn't really going as I had hoped.

Leanne: Thanks for volunteering, Chris. Let's follow the protocol and see what happens. You'll have four minutes to share with us where you are with your work. You can use the sentence completion sheet you filled out to help you share in a succinct manner. Four minutes goes quickly. I'll keep time. Let's begin.

Chris: Okay, I'm ready. Well, as you already know, I'm extremely intrigued with technology. Most recently I've become fascinated with blogging as a teaching tool. Every year, when I teach the novel *Moby Dick,* I'm not entirely happy with the nature of the discussions we have in class. Sometimes I just don't know how to get students to participate more, dig a little deeper, and use higher-level thinking skills as we discuss the novel in class. I thought it might be interesting to see if blogging could make a difference. Therefore, with your help, I set out to understand how Weblogs might support or hinder my students' discussion during class. My guiding questions for my PLC work, which you all so brilliantly helped me craft a few months ago, were as follows: What happens when I add a blogging component to my unit on *Moby Dick* with my eleventh grade honors/ AP class? In what ways does blogging contribute to my students' understandings of the novel? What is the relationship between blogging and the application of higher-order thinking skills to literature discussion?

(Continued)

(Continued)

Leanne: You have one minute remaining.

Chris: As you may recall, from our action learning plan meeting, I took action by setting up a blogging site for my class to use and collected data by printing out and reading all of the posts, giving out a questionnaire to my students about blogging, and saving every bit of paper produced by me and my students during my teaching of *Moby Dick.* So far, one thing I'm discovering from my data is that students are posting but not necessarily responding to each other's posts. It's like they use the blog to dump their thoughts out, but no one responds to each other. Another thing I'm discovering is that there is great variety in the quality of responses by the students. A few responses are really thoughtful as well as thought provoking, but most responses are so general I have to wonder if the student even read the assigned chapter. It's definitely not working like I thought it would.

Leanne: Okay, Chris, I'm going to have to stop you there. It's been four minutes.

Narrator: Leanne addressed the group.

Leanne: In the next three minutes, we get to ask Chris clarifying questions. As a reminder, these are questions that have factual answers.

Narrator: During those three minutes, members of the group posed the following four questions that Chris responded to:

- Can you remind us about what the site looks like and how it operates?
- What instructions did you give you students about how to use the blog site?
- Are there instructions for the students on the site itself?
- Have you ensured that all of your students have access to computers to participate?

After Chris's response to the fourth question, Leanne jumped in.

Leanne: Although I know we may have a few more clarifying questions we might want Chris to answer, it's time for us to shift gears now and ask probing questions. As a reminder, probing questions are worded to help Chris dig deeper into his thinking and his data analysis. One thing to be careful of is disguising a suggestion as a probing question or disguising your own thinking or opinion as a probing question by starting out with a phrase such as, Did you think of trying . . .? or Did you ever consider that . . .? At this point, we do not want to offer suggestions to Chris or impose our own thinking on him. Rather, we want to ask questions to help us delve a little deeper into his inquiry and his data. We'll have the opportunity to make suggestions and share our thinking in the next step of this protocol.

Narrator: Joan began with the first probing question.

Joan: What are you looking for when you review the postings?

Chris: Well, I'm looking for a couple things. First, I'm looking at the responses, kind of with a Bloom's Taxonomy eye. What I mean by that is are they analyzing, synthesizing, and evaluating in their responses to my blog prompts? I'm also looking not just at how I might categorize their responses using Bloom's Taxonomy but looking at their responses for how they might get scored on Florida Writes, our lovely state test. Of course I want these students to do their very best on this. And as I read their responses, I also can't help but consider how that response might be scored on the AP exam too. I haven't been happy with what I've seen so far.

Narrator: There was a brief pause, and Sherri jumped in.

Sherri: I remember reading *Moby Dick* in high school, and it was very difficult reading. I can't say I have fond memories of it. I'm wondering why you chose *Moby Dick*? Are they required to read that text?

Chris: Well, no, they're not required to read it. We have a list of books from the state that we can choose from, but you don't have to read every book on the list. I chose it because I consider myself a child of the sea. I grew up myself not far from the ocean. I love fishing and adventure stories, and I like the writing style of the author, so I thought it would be a great novel for the kids. I know it's a challenging read. There's a good deal of internal dialogue the kids have to get through. There's usually a bunch of groans when I first introduce the book. The kids give me a look as if to say, Are you kidding me? But I like the book, and I think it's good for them!

Sherri: Did you ever think that it might be difficult for the students to relate to this novel, and because they can't relate and it provides some difficult content, their blogs aren't up to par?

Leanne: Hold on a minute. Let me stop everyone for a second. Sherri, that's one of those disguised questions—you're really giving Chris your own ideas in the way that question is phrased. Hold on to your own thoughts for the next step, and let's keep our questions open. Could anyone reword Sherri's question so it's a probing question and not a suggestion for Chris?

Mickey: I'll give it a try. Chris, what factors might contribute to your students' ability (or inability) to produce quality blog entries?

Chris: Wow, that's a great question, Mickey. One factor could be the direction for the blog assignment itself. If the directions aren't clear, that could affect the quality. Another thing I suppose is me being explicit about what I'm

(Continued)

(Continued)

looking for in their entries. Since I'm new to using blogging, I think I had in my head what I wanted to see, but I'm not sure I communicated it well to the students. I guess I also might see more quality blog activity if the content wasn't so difficult, but that's a catch-22 situation. I thought the blog activity would be good just for that reason—it would give the students yet another venue to deconstruct a difficult text. I'll have to think about that some more.

Narrator: Leanne took a turn probing.

Leanne: Chris, you said that one of the things you are looking for in their prompts is higher-order thinking skills. What have you done with your students to help them understand higher-order thinking?

Chris: Well, I've done some instruction with topic sentences and various activities to help them build on those sentences.

Narrator: Chris stopped and thought for a minute.

Chris: I don't think I'm answering your question. In reality, Leanne, I don't think I've done much to scaffold their learning and application of higher-order thinking from other class activities to the blog activity.

Joan: What implications does what you are learning from your data have for your teaching?

Chris: I am definitely seeing adaptations I could make to the ways I designed the site so it is more effective. I also just assumed that because these kids were eleventh-grade honors/AP students that they would really take off with the blogging, you know, like a duck takes to water. Being bright students, I also assumed that their blogs would be so thought provoking that they would automatically be compelled to respond to each other. Those were naive assumptions on my part. You would think that after so many years teaching I would have known better. I can't just teach the content of *Moby Dick*. I have to teach the technology too. I need to teach them what constitutes a quality blog entry and perhaps not only what constitutes a quality blog entry but a quality response to a peer's blog.

Narrator: Leanne finished up with the last question . . .

Leanne: Chris, we have time for only one more question, and I think a good one to finish up might be this: What new questions do you have?

Chris: There's a lot of things swirling around in my head right now, but one thing that's coming to mind is the development of a rubric for blog responses. If I developed a rubric, I'd want to know the relationship between the rubric and the students' ability to produce blog responses that are indicative of higher-order thinking.

Leanne: Okay, thanks Chris. At this point, we're going to move on to the next step in the protocol. Chris, we are now going to discuss your inquiry with each other, as if you weren't in the room. You are to remain silent. You might want to take notes as we talk. You also might want to scoot your chair back a little from our circle and turn away from us just a tad to help you resist the urge to contribute to the discussion.

Narrator: Chris scooted his chair back from the group as Leanne suggested and took out his notepad, ready to write. Leanne continued by addressing the group . . .

Leanne: We are going to talk about Chris's data for six minutes. We should discuss questions such as these: What did we hear? What didn't we hear that we think might be relevant? What assumptions seem to be operating? Do any data not seem to fit with the presenter's analysis? What might be some additional ways to look at the presenter's data? What we're trying to do is deepen Chris's analysis. And Sherri, here's the time you could make suggestions.

Joan: I hear Chris say that when analyzing his students' blog entries, he was looking for the higher levels of Bloom's Taxonomy in their responses, and most of the responses were not at those higher-order thinking levels. I wonder if Chris made this statement based on his impressions over time or if he actually sorted his data by Bloom's Taxonomy level. He might want to actually sort the blog entries into the categories of knowledge, comprehension, application, analysis, synthesis, and evaluation. He also might want to sort his blog prompts into these categories as well. He might discover some interesting things by sorting his data this way. Maybe it's not as bad as he thinks. Maybe the prompts themselves aren't all higher-level questions. Are knowledge, comprehension, and application questions inherently bad? Especially for a difficult novel like *Moby Dick*, I would imagine the students would need to spend some time in the knowledge, comprehension, and application domains before they are able to discuss the text at a higher level.

Mickey: I also hear Chris say that he was looking at the responses for how they might get scored on the Florida Writes and the AP exam. That was puzzling to me, because I heard nothing in Chris's wondering statements that had to do with student writing. In all the discussions we had about his inquiry at previous meetings, I never remember hearing anything about Florida Writes or the AP exam. Did you?

(All members of the PLC shake their heads no.)

This writing thing is totally new. He needs to return to his guiding questions to remind himself of what he set out to look for in the first place. He

(Continued)

(Continued)

didn't ask, "How does blogging help students prepare for Florida Writes and the AP test?"

Joan: Along with that, I was thinking that his students were perceiving the blog site like they might perceive Facebook—or even Twitter. They write in a much more informal way in these venues. Why would you expect they'd write like they would for an exam on a blog site?

(All members of the PLC nod in agreement.)

Leanne: I think an important part of his data analysis is going to be looking very closely at all of his lesson plans and everything that went into designing the blog site itself. He might want to turn his gaze to focus on the setup: What did I learn from the way I set it all up? What worked? What didn't?

Mickey: I didn't hear him talk at all about the questionnaires. Did he look at them yet, or did he only look at the blog entries themselves?

Sherri: All right, I've been quiet long enough. I have to come back to his choice of *Moby Dick.* I can't imagine that's an easy book for the kids to relate to, and that certainly could inhibit their responses. Maybe Chris should try a more accessible novel for eleventh graders in the future. I know they're honors/AP students, but *Moby Dick*? There may be better choices on that list from the state.

Mickey: Does Chris have to be the one to pick from that list? What would happen if he did a little two-minute commercial on each book on the list, and then his students could vote on the one they want to read.

Joan: Or each individual student could pick the book he or she wanted, and Chris could make book blog groups. Does everyone in the class have to be reading the same book at the same time?

Narrator: There was a pause while everyone thought. Leanne took this opportunity to look down at her watch and broke the silence with . . .

Leanne: We have two minutes left.

Joan: I think Chris uncovered some of his own assumptions when he was speaking. For instance, Chris noted that just because they were bright kids, he thought they'd take to blogging like ducks take to water.

Leanne: He also thought they'd respond to each other naturally.

Sherri: I think this is one thing he might take into consideration in the design of the blog and his directions for its use. Maybe the kids need to be required not just to post but to respond to at least three classmate's blogs by a certain date . . . or something like that.

Joan: I worry that Chris is beating up on himself too hard for making some assumptions about advanced learners. He even started out by saying that he didn't think he was learning much from his inquiry since the blogging was not going as he had planned. Well, gosh, I think he's learning an incredible amount. One thing he is learning is that we all make assumptions based on ability when we plan our lessons. Sometimes the assumptions we make limit our planning. This could even be one of the claims he makes from this exploration of his teaching . . . something like, "It is important for teachers to uncover hidden assumptions they hold about their learners that may interfere with the teacher's ability to introduce something new to the class." I know I was thinking about that as he was talking. His work helped me look at myself and the assumptions I make as well. The practice of uncovering our assumptions is a good reminder for us all!

Narrator: Leanne agreed.

Leanne: I think that's really powerful. It's important to remember that PLC work isn't about finding a new strategy and reporting on the miraculous difference it made to teaching. Although that does happen occasionally, more often than not, teaching is just too complex to have any one new thing we might try in the classroom as teachers lead to dramatic improvement for every learner in a short period of time. But that doesn't mean that there isn't tons of learning that happens in our PLC work. It seems like Chris has a lot of rich learning to report on! And with that comment, I'm going to have to call time and ask Chris to come back and join us in the circle. Chris, you now have three minutes to reflect on what you heard us say.

Chris: Wow, this was incredible. I have three full pages of notes. Let me just share a few things. First, I really like the idea of sorting the blog entries and prompts by taxonomy level. I haven't done that yet. I do think that would be an interesting exercise. I was thinking it's all about higher-level thinking, and that's the only valuable blog response to have. Once I sort, I think I might find some value in using the blog for knowledge, comprehension, and application as well as analysis, synthesis, and evaluation. I'm going to go through my data again and look closely at what exactly is happening at each of those levels as well as how the lower-level responses might be building blocks for the higher-level responses.

I also want to say that you're right on about the Florida Writes and the AP test. That did just seem to creep into my work. I think that probably happened because we're getting close to the end of the year, and of course, just like everyone, those tests and my students' performance on them is ever present on my mind. This wasn't the focus of the work I set out to do, though, so I need to let that one go. There's no need to sort my data by the score a response like that would be received on the exams.

I do think there's something to the students' application of Facebook and Twitter behaviors to the blog space. I think I even might want to do a few

(Continued)

(Continued)

interviews with certain students to see if they perceive my blog site in the same ways they perceive all those social networking sites—wow, that could have some powerful implications for how I adapt my blog site in the future as well as the instructions I give about participation on the site.

And I have administered and collected the questionnaires, but I just glanced at them. I have to go back and look at the questionnaires more closely.

(Leanne motions to Chris by pointing to her watch indicated that time is almost up.)

I have a lot more to say, but Leanne is giving me the time signal, so I just want to thank everyone. I have to admit that I was really skeptical about this whole protocol thing and data analysis at first, but this session has been incredibly helpful. I have so much to consider! Thanks.

Leanne: *(smiling)* Thank you, Chris. You were brave to present first. We will now take just two minutes to reflect on the process.

Mickey: For lack of a better word, this was really cool. The protocol worked well. It kept us focused and on topic, and the time moved quickly.

Sherri: I think it's hard to distinguish between suggestions and probing questions. I know I had a hard time with that, but when Mickey rephrased my question, I did see that difference and why it is important to make sure a question is a true probing question and not a suggestion disguised as a probing question.

Leanne: It's not easy to develop good probing questions, but it's a skill we'll all get better at with time.

Joan: It felt a little weird talking about Chris as if he wasn't in the room when he was sitting right next to me.

Narrator: Everyone chuckled.

Chris: You think it felt weird to you—I'm glad I took Leanne's suggestion and pulled away from the circle a bit. There were so many times I wanted to say something when you were discussing me. I'm glad the protocol wouldn't let me though. I learned so much by just listening!

Leanne: That's time! Let's take a quick five-minute break and then Joan, why don't you present next?

Narrator: The members of the learning community relaxed. Chris helped himself to a second brownie, Sherri went to the restroom, Mickey purchased a soda, and Joan engaged in some quiet conversation with Leanne as they waited for the others to return. While they momentarily went their separate ways, each member of the learning community had experienced the power of protocols and data analysis that afternoon. They eagerly awaited the next round.

Questions for Discussion

1. This chapter names three different protocols specifically designed to structure PLC conversation about data ("ATLAS—Looking at Data" protocol, the "Data Driven Dialogue" protocol, and "Data Mining Protocol"). Retrieve these protocols from the SRI website (www.school reforminitiative.org/protocols) to compare and contrast with one another.

   • How are these protocols similar?
   • How are these protocols different?
   • In what situations might each of these protocols be useful in a PLC to structure conversation as a part of formative data analysis?
   • How and when could you use each of these protocols in your own PLC work?

2. At the end of their summative data analysis meeting, Kevin's PLC was getting ready to share a short presentation about the work of their PLC and what they had learned together that school year about culturally responsive teaching.

   • Why is it important to share the learning of a PLC with others?
   • In addition to faculty meeting presentations, what are some other ways a PLC might share their work with other professionals both inside and outside their school?

3. In the reader's theater, Leanne helped PLC members distinguish between probing questions and suggestions that are disguised as probing questions.

   • What probing questions did the group pose to Chris?
   • What characteristics do these probing questions share?
   • In what ways do these probing question differ from suggestions phrased as questions?
   • What suggestions did PLC members name for Chris to consider during Step 4 of the protocol when Chris was not participating but simply listening to the group discuss his data?
   • What are some reasons is it important to "hold off" on the provision of suggestions to PLC members as they think about their work?
   • What are some reasons for the presenter *not* to participate in the discussion when PLC members are discussing their thinking about the presenter's data?

4. Imagine the same PLC meeting with Chris, Leanne, Mickey, Joan, and Sherri transpiring without the use of a protocol. What might the meeting have looked like, and how might the conversation have been different without the use of the data analysis protocol?

6

Making PLC
Learning Public

WHAT MAKING PLC LEARNING
PUBLIC IS AND WHY IT'S IMPORTANT

In some ways, it may seem odd to think about making your professional learning community (PLC) learning public as a separate component of PLC work. You might think that this happens inherently as a result of what PLC work is all about in the first place—making your practice public by sharing it and learning from it with others over time. Individual members of your PLC have been making their practice public to each other throughout the school year. Yet, like the process of data analysis, which consists of formative and summative activities, so is the process of PLC sharing.

Formative sharing happens automatically as PLC members communicate issues, tensions, problems, and dilemmas with one another and explore these through the processes described in this book. Formative sharing can be defined as teachers collaborating with one another within the PLC to share and investigate their own teaching practice together. However, as critically important as formative sharing is, as a PLC nears the end of its work, it is important to engage in summative sharing as well. This summative sharing allows others outside your PLC to benefit from the hard work your group has engaged in over time. Summative sharing can be defined as teachers collaborating with one another to prepare and communicate the results of their PLC work with other professionals.

The following short vignette demonstrates the importance of devoting time to summative sharing of your PLC work with others:

> A young man took his thirteen-year old son to the lake. He was looking forward to spending the beautiful spring day making fond memories with his son, who was growing much too quickly for his father's comfort. The weather was perfect—the sun was warm, and the air was fresh with just a little nip of cold remaining from the long winter months. Being it was early spring, they had the entire park to themselves—not another family was in sight.
>
> The day was going just as he had planned. After the perfect morning canoe trip, they headed to the shore and ate their picnic lunch. After lunch, the man gazed out to the shore and admired the peaceful, calm lake before him. His thoughts drifted to replaying the wonderful morning he and his son had shared together, and he was feeling quite proud of the all-day excursion he had planned for his son during these delicate teenage years. It couldn't have been going any better. Just then, his thoughts were abruptly interrupted by his child's voice. "Dad, I'm bored."
>
> The man was taken aback—stunned that his son could feel boredom in the face of the beautiful glassy-still lake before them. "How could you be bored, Son?" his father queried. "The lake is so beautiful—peaceful and still."
>
> "That's just it, Dad," his son replied. "You might see beauty, but I see stagnation. His son's comment provided a stark reality check for the man. They had sat for too long, and he needed to think quickly to save the perfect day he had planned with his son from spoiling.
>
> "Son," his father said, "I think it's time to put an end to the stagnation. You see all of these rocks along the shore? Have I ever told you I was my town's rock-skipping champion when I was a kid? I can give you a few pointers and teach you how to skip rocks like nobody's business!"
>
> The teenaged boy looked skeptical, "Aw, Dad. I'm too old for that stuff."
>
> "You're never too old to have fun and to learn something new. Now watch me."
>
> The man searched for the perfect rock on the lakeshore and tossed it into the water. It skipped three times before it finally fell to the bottom. Its hops across the water's surface created an interesting pattern of ripples.
>
> While the boy didn't want to admit it, he was impressed. He watched his father throw five more rocks in quick succession—one even skipped four times! He decided since no one was in sight to see him, it would be okay to participate with his father.

They threw for an hour, his father teaching him technique and form to get as many skips as possible out of each rock. As they tossed stone after stone, the clear, stagnant lake became alive with small swells, ridges, and swirls. Some of the ripples even reached the shore of the lake! The man was once again proud of his quick thinking— the stone-throwing game had saved the day.

Like the stones laying on the lakeshore that have no chance of affecting the still water unless tossed in by the man and his teenaged son, if you do not share the learning of your PLC with others, the impact of that learning is limited only to PLC membership. Unless what is learned by an individual PLC is tossed into broader professional conversation and dialogue, that learning has only limited potential to disturb the status quo of educational practices. However, if you do share, the learning of your PLC can create a ripple effect, beginning with the teachers in your PLC themselves, their immediate vicinity (the students in PLC members' classrooms), and emanating out to a school, and maybe even a district. Hence, although the notions of making practice public and sharing it with others is embedded within the PLC to begin with, it is also important to make sharing visible by naming it as one important component of PLC work.

In sum, as you engage in PLC work over the course of a school year, there will be a lot of learning that transpires, both for individual members of the PLC as well as for your PLC as a whole. It's important to be generous with that learning, sharing it with your administration and other colleagues at your school, perhaps even parents and students and district level administration as well, and potentially with other teaching professionals outside of your school and district. In this way, the PLC work has the capacity to influence and inform not only the members of the PLC who have partaken in this form of professional learning with one another but others as well.

HOW TO MAKE PLC LEARNING PUBLIC

The most prevalent way we have seen PLCs make their learning public is at a school's faculty meeting. If an entire school has been engaged in PLC work over the course of a school year, the principal may even designate one faculty meeting toward the end of the year to be devoted to reports of the learning that has occurred in each individual PLC. Likewise, different PLCs may share "progress reports" on their work with the entire school faculty additionally throughout the school year as their work unfolds and warrants a larger sharing with the entire school community.

In addition to faculty meetings, we have also seen PLC work shared in larger district and staff meetings, depending on the nature of the work and the potential it has to affect a district at large. Some PLCs even create a blog to capture their work and their learning over time for a broader education audience. Finally, we have also seen some PLCs present their learning at local, state, and national conferences.

WHAT MIGHT SHARING THE WORK OF YOUR PLC LOOK LIKE?

Sometimes members of a PLC share their work more informally with a group, but sometimes it can be useful to create a PowerPoint presentation to accompany the oral telling of a PLC story. PowerPoint presentations can be very effectively used as an aid to help you communicate the essence of your PLC experience and what you learned as a result. A number of wonderful websites exist that can help you think about the essentials of an effective PowerPoint presentation. The most important thing to remember about creating an effective PowerPoint presentation is to keep it simple! Remember, the PowerPoint is not the presenter—you are! The PowerPoint slides serve as a tool to enhance or emphasize points you wish to make about your PLC work, not to tell every single detail of every single PLC meeting you have had over the course of the school year. Some of the most important aspects of keeping your PowerPoint simple appear here:

Effective PowerPoint Presentations—Keep It Simple!

Limit

- Information to the essentials
- Number of slides
- Special effects
- Fancy fonts

Use

- Key phrases
- Large font sizes (between 18 and 48 point is the general range)
- Colors that contrast
- Clip art and graphics to balance the slide—not overwhelm it

An example of a PowerPoint presentation completed by a PLC is shared at the end of this chapter. While it is difficult to glean detail about a presentation by just looking at presentation slides and not actually hearing the talk, review this presentation to gain insights into the ways a PowerPoint presentation of PLC work might unfold.

In this case, eleven teachers at P. K. Yonge Developmental Research School (Christy Barba, Kelly Barrett, Mayra Codero, Christy Gabbard, Tanya Kort, Eric Lemstrom, Mickey MacDonald, Mark Magura, Cody Miller, Kristin Weller, and Kate Yurko) had formed a learning community at the start of the school year based on their shared dissatisfaction with current grading practice at their school and interest in standards-based grading. Early in their PLC work, the group read and discussed literature on standards-based grading, defined as assessing students based only on their mastery of learning goals rather than determining grades based on other variables such as completion of homework, grades on formative assessments, and class participation (O'Connor, 2007; Reeves, 2007). The following overarching question guided the learning of this PLC: What are the implications of changing our practice to incorporate elements of standards-based grading? To investigate this overarching question, the teachers in this PLC developed five subquestions that different individuals or subsets of individuals within this PLC explored and shared with the group as their work extended over the course of the school year.

At the end of the school year, the director of the school invited these teachers to share the work of their PLC at a faculty luncheon. To provide an overview, the teachers created the PowerPoint presentation that appears at the end of this chapter using the first five slides (after the title slide) to explain to their colleagues what standards-based grading is and why it holds potential for positively affecting student work and student learning. Following this overview, slides 7 and 8 stated the PLC overarching question as well as an overview of how this particular PLC organized their work together during the school year. Slides 9 through 13 introduced the five subquestions explored by individuals and subsets of individuals within this PLC. Slide 14 was organizational, naming each member of the PLC and the number of a table they would sit at where faculty could come to discuss what was learned from the investigation of each individual subquestion after their whole-group presentation had ended. Slides 15 and 16 each contained three bulleted points that captured the big ideas the PLC learned across all of the subquestion members had explored. Finally, the last two slides captured where they were headed next year in their PLC work and included an invitation to other faculty members to join the work of their PLC in the coming school year.

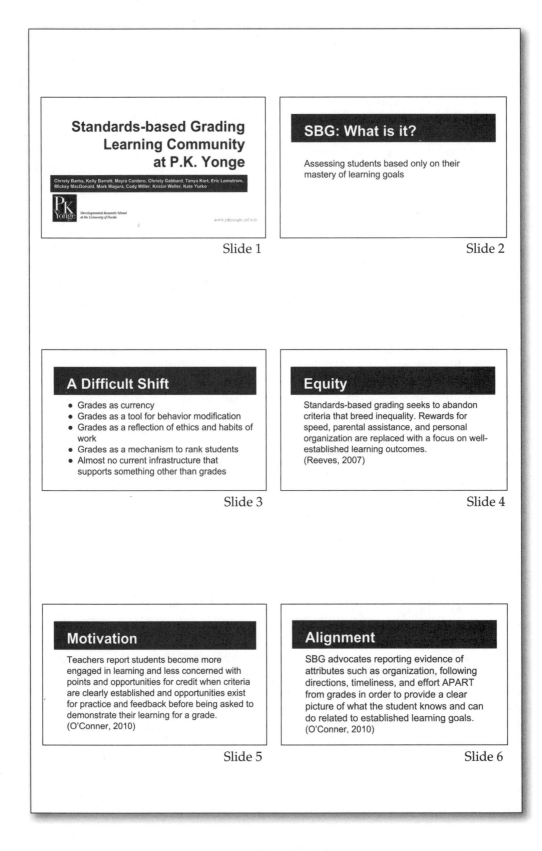

Standards-based Grading Learning Community at P.K. Yonge

Christy Barba, Kelly Barrett, Mayra Cordero, Christy Gabbard, Tanya Kort, Eric Lemstrom, Mickey MacDonald, Mark Magura, Cody Miller, Kristin Weller, Kate Yurko

P.K. Yonge
Developmental Research School
at the University of Florida
www.pkyonge.ufl.edu

Slide 1

SBG: What is it?

Assessing students based only on their mastery of learning goals

Slide 2

A Difficult Shift

- Grades as currency
- Grades as a tool for behavior modification
- Grades as a reflection of ethics and habits of work
- Grades as a mechanism to rank students
- Almost no current infrastructure that supports something other than grades

Slide 3

Equity

Standards-based grading seeks to abandon criteria that breed inequality. Rewards for speed, parental assistance, and personal organization are replaced with a focus on well-established learning outcomes. (Reeves, 2007)

Slide 4

Motivation

Teachers report students become more engaged in learning and less concerned with points and opportunities for credit when criteria are clearly established and opportunities exist for practice and feedback before being asked to demonstrate their learning for a grade. (O'Conner, 2010)

Slide 5

Alignment

SBG advocates reporting evidence of attributes such as organization, following directions, timeliness, and effort APART from grades in order to provide a clear picture of what the student knows and can do related to established learning goals. (O'Conner, 2010)

Slide 6

PLC Work & Guiding Question

Practical exploration of the way in which grades currently work in our classes.

What are the implications of changing practice to incorporate elements of standards-based grading?

Slide 7

Logistics of Our PLC

- 11 teachers volunteered
- Frustrated with what grades communicated to students and parents
- Optimistic about changing simple classroom policies to improve learning
- Each determined a question for exploration specific to context

Slide 8

Subquestions

Q1: Mayra Codero

In what ways does the elimination of a participation category impact student content knowledge achievement?

Slide 9

Subquestions

Q2 - Tanya Kort, Eric Lemstrom, Cody Miller, and Kate Yurko

Once we codify retake and revision procedures, which students will take advantage of the procedures, and what progress will they make?

Slide 10

Subquestions

Q3: Kristin Weller and Mark Magura

What structures, other than grades, ensure our students are motivated to complete assignments in a timely manner to help them master learning targets and perform well on assessments?

In what ways can we convince students that completing voluntary homework is essential to their academic success?

Slide 11

Subquestions

Q4: Mickey MacDonald and Christy Barba

In what ways can reassessment practices be structured to support student learning in a Standards-Based Biology classroom?

How does a teacher, within the day to day context of teaching, develop reassessment pieces and interventions for students who need additional engagement with content to achieve mastery?

Slide 12

Subquestions

Q5: Kelly Barrett

How does a more accurate representation of student's skill and strategy development impact grades in the skills assessment category?

Will a more accurate representation of student's skill and strategy development impact student effort on a daily basis?

Slide 13

Opportunity to Learn More

Table 1 - Barba and MacDonald
Table 2 - Kort, Lemstrom, Miller, and Yurko
Table 3 - Kelly Barrett
Table 4 - Mayra Cordero
Table 5 - Magura and Weller

Slide 14

Preliminary "Big Ideas"

- Reassessment opportunities improve student learning significantly for all types of learners.
- To be most successful, support for reassessment should be provided in the regular instructional period.
- Constant communication between teachers and students is ESSENTIAL for student success.

Slide 15

Preliminary "Big Ideas" cont.

- Exposing students to the relation between assessment scores and assignment completion shows students the relevance of completing assigned work.
- SBG is an effective tool to identify students in need of tiered support.
- A non-grade structure to address poor academic behaviors must be established to make SBG effective.

Slide 16

Our PLC Work Continues…

Year 1
School Year 2014-15
Ken O'Connor's Fixes:
- *Practices that distort achievement (or accurately reflect learning)*
- *Investigating grade calculations*

Year 2
School Year 2015-16
Ken O'Connor's Fixes:
- *Fixes for low-quality or poorly organized evidence*
- *Fixes that support learning*

Slide 17

Next Year

Please consider joining us as we continue to explore the implications of changing assessment practice to incorporate elements of standards-based grading

Slide 18

Questions for Discussion

1. What do you believe to be the value of making the work and learning of your PLC public?

2. What do you believe to be some of the challenges associated with making the work and learning of your PLC public?

3. How might your PLC share its work and learning with others?

7

Essential Elements of Healthy PLCs

As we approach the end of this book, you've now read about what a professional learning community (PLC) is and how PLC work might transpire over the course of a school year. We covered how to get started, determine a direction and plan for your PLC, analyze data, and share your PLC work with others. While each component of PLC work shared in the previous chapters serve as important "benchmarks" for the ways PLC work transpires over the course of a school year, there are several essential elements of PLC work that must be embedded within and across each benchmark discussed in the previous chapters. These essential elements converge to create and maintain what we refer to as a *healthy PLC*.

While it may initially seem odd to use a term most often associated with the field of medicine—*healthy*—to modify an entity most often associated with the field of education—PLC—our teaching profession shares a great deal of similarities with the medical profession. Both professions have recently acknowledged the importance of collaboration between professionals within their fields. The medical field has recently shifted toward using a team-based approach to enhance patient care. This is particularly true in hospitals, where doctors, nurses, dietitians, physical therapists, social workers, and discharge planners all collaborate to share professional knowledge that ensures quality care. This multidisciplinary, team-based approach brings a diverse and specialized group of professionals together. The medical team members need to pay attention to their patient, listen attentively to each other, communicate, and problem solve together. When these professionals know how to effectively communicate with other members of the health team, they are able to provide higher-quality patient care.

Much like the medical team who is responsible for providing high-quality patient care, PLCs are composed of a team of teachers who are responsible for working together to provide the highest quality student care by improving teaching and learning. This requires the creation of a collaborative culture where teachers develop PLCs that will be powerful enough to promote student learning and school improvement (Garmston, 2007). Garmston (2007) reminds us that creating a culture of collaboration "rather than continuing to work in a culture of isolation represents a significant change within schools that must be supported. Systems successful in improving student learning are characterized by articulated norms and values, a focus on student learning, reflective dialogue, collaborative practice, and deprivatization of teaching" (p. 21). Just as the members of the medical team collaborate to keep a laser-like focus on patient care, teachers in a PLC develop a collaborative culture by keeping a laser-like focus on student learning.

The laser-like focus on the patient for the medical team is twofold. First, the medical team provides well-patient care by seeing patients for regular checkups and assessing that all systems in the body are functioning properly and working together to ensure the overall health of the patient. Second, the medical team sees patients when they are ill, diagnoses the problem, and prescribes a course of treatment to bring the patient back to good health again. In a similar fashion, the laser-like focus on student learning for the PLC is obtained by using the essential elements we will discuss in this final chapter to reflect on the work of your PLC to be sure "all systems are healthy" and, when it is not functioning optimally, prescribe a course of action to bring your PLC back to good health again.

Hence, we end this book by naming ten essential elements of PLC work that are important to weave into the fabric of the being of a PLC. Many of these elements were highly visible and named as a part of the PLC work benchmarks that were described in the previous chapters you have read, while some of these elements were less visible in the previous chapters and some are introduced here for the first time. Whether review or new, we believe that placing all of these elements together in one place at the end of this book can help you continually assess the health of your PLC and, like the medical team, work together with the other members of your PLC to diagnose any problems that need attention in the ways your PLC is functioning, treat the problem, and return your PLC to optimal health once again! These ten elements are summarized in Figure 7.1 and include (1) establishing and maintaining a vision, (2) building trust, (3) understanding and embracing collaboration, (4) appreciating diversity, (5) becoming critical friends, (6) engaging in work "in between," (7) documenting learning, (8) using multiple forms and types of data, (9) gaining comfort with change, and (10) working with school leadership.

TEN ESSENTIAL ELEMENTS OF HEALTHY PLCs

Essential Element #1: Healthy PLCs Establish a Vision That Creates Momentum for Their Learning

According to Thomas Sergiovanni (1994), "Community building must become the heart of any school improvement effort. . . . It requires us to think community, believe in community, and practice community" (p. 95). At the start of your PLC work, it is important to take the time to collaboratively establish and maintain a school improvement vision for the PLC work you are about to begin. This can be accomplished through the development of a guiding question to drive your PLC work. Developing a vision is essential for establishing a collegial context for your shared work.

Figure 7.1   Top Ten List: Essential Elements of a Healthy PLC

Healthy PLCs do the following:

1. Establish a vision that creates momentum for their learning.

2. Build trust among group members.

3. Understand and embrace collaboration.

4. Encourage, recognize, and appreciate diversity within the group.

5. Promote the development of critical friends.

6. Pay attention to the work "in between" meetings.

7. Hold the group accountable for and document their learning.

8. Have a comprehensive view of what constitutes data and are willing to consider all forms and types of data throughout their PLC work.

9. Understand change and acknowledge the discomfort it may bring to some PLC members.

10. Work with their building administrators.

Essential Element #2: Healthy PLCs
Build Trust Among Group Members

Educational scholars have long noted the critical importance of building trust among the adults within the school building and the correlation between trusting relationships and successful school improvement efforts. For example, Bryk and Schneider (2002) state the following:

> Relational trust does not directly affect student learning. Rather, trust fosters a set of organizational conditions, some structural and others social-psychological, that make it more conducive for individuals to initiate and sustain the kinds of activities necessary to affect productivity improvements. (p. 116)

Michael Fullan (1999) also notes, "The quality of relationships is central to success [of school improvement efforts]. Success is only possible if organizational members develop trust and compassion for each other" (p. 37). As a result, building trust within your group is an essential component of PLC work.

Essential Element #3: Healthy PLCs
Understand and Embrace Collaboration

Hunter, Bailey, and Taylor (1995) suggest that when it comes to collaboration, "One + one + one + one = five." This unconventional mathematics is what happens when a group of teachers work together toward a common objective. When people work together, they create synergy that helps move the group toward fulfilling the shared purpose. To date, teachers' work has been fairly autonomous, as classroom teachers have typically worked independently in their individual classrooms. As a member of a PLC, you shift from working independently to working collaboratively with a group of professionals dedicated to learning with and from one another to become the very best teachers they can be for every student they teach.

Essential Element #4: Healthy PLCs Encourage,
Recognize, and Appreciate Diversity Within the Group

Individual members of a PLC come with diverse values, skills, knowledge, beliefs, philosophies, experiences, expertise, and perspectives. It is this type of diversity that generates energy for change as well as the disequilibrium necessary for learning (Jacobs, 2007; Lambert, Collay, Dietz, Kent, & Richert, 1996). PLC members recognize that membership diversity is something to both celebrate and plan for. Without diversity, your PLC can become entrenched in groupthink, which can become highly unproductive and may just perpetuate the status quo rather than move your group forward. Groupthink often results in hasty decisions, where individual doubts are set aside and ideas are not questioned. If your group members can recognize the importance of diverse group membership to their learning as well as the importance of allowing members both inside and outside of the group to participate, the PLC is likely to thrive.

According to Cushman (1999), PLCs do the following:

> [They] are highly strategic and purposeful about seeking and using outside information, resources, expertise, and collaborations. Ideas, information, and people constantly move across their boundaries with the "outside." (p. 42)

Each PLC group member needs to value and make sure that diverse voices are heard. Each group member also needs to be sure that diverse perspectives are garnered from outside sources when the group lacks diverse knowledge and perspective. It is important to identify critical junctures where bringing external expertise to your group will benefit teacher learning and the direction of your group's work. This may mean that you spend time reading research-based articles from educational journals, observing other teachers in other schools, visiting a specialist, or listening to a guest speaker from the district who has strong knowledge in a particular area.

Essential Element #5: Healthy PLCs Promote the Development of Critical Friends

According to Peter Senge (2007), developing capabilities for real conversation is not easy.

> Most of what passes for conversation in contemporary society is more like a Ping-Pong game than true talking and thinking together. Each individual tosses his or her view at the other. Each then responds. Often, we are preparing our response before we have even heard the other person's view. In effect, we are "taking our shot" before we have even received the other's ball. "Learningful" conversations require individuals capable of reflecting on their own thinking.

The challenge is figuring out how to make these kinds of "learningful" conversations happen within your PLC. Meaningful and practice-changing PLC work requires your group to communicate with each other in ways that promote collegiality and results in teacher learning. This type of communication is referred to as critical friendship. The *critical* in critical friends does not mean being critical in a judgmental way about each others' practice but rather being willing to engage in courageous conversations that are critical to everyone's learning and that allow critical insights about teaching and learning to emerge. This type of friendship and conversation, often structured by the use of protocols, is essential within a PLC.

Essential Element #6: Healthy PLCs Pay Attention to the Work "In Between" Meetings

In order for educators to collaborate together with the goal of learning about their practice, PLC membership requires you to work outside and in between the PLC meetings. This work outside the PLC meetings is equally important to the success of your PLC. Your learning in between PLC meetings provides opportunities for you to test out your ideas and reshape your practices. The work in between requires you and your PLC group members to implement innovative ideas and practices with support as well as collect data to better understand how these innovations are affecting students. In-between work might include completing readings; journaling; trying new teaching strategies; collecting student work; observing others and having others observe you; reviewing data; and preparing to present issues, dilemmas, tensions, and problems that emerge in your own teaching practice for discussion with and feedback from PLC members.

In addition, there is a variety of related professional development tools that can be used to stimulate and support learning in between PLC meetings. In another book we have written, *Powerful Professional Development* (Yendol-Hoppey & Dana, 2010), we identify a number of job-embedded learning tools that can help you implement and assess the ideas that emerge from your PLCs. These include (1) research in action, (2) co-teaching, (3) teacher research, and (4) the use of a variety of coaching models. When PLC members extend their work from the group meeting to classroom implementation, these tools help deepen professional learning and the work of the PLC.

Essential Element #7: Healthy PLCs Hold the Group Accountable for and Document Their Learning

One of your roles as a PLC member is to help document your group's collective work. Documentation is essential as the data allow your group to share their work with those outside of the PLC. By being able to document success in terms of changes for students, you will be better positioned to acquire outside funds, compete for scarce internal resources, and perhaps even influence education policy.

Essential Element #8: Healthy PLCs Have a Comprehensive View of What Constitutes Data and Are Willing to Consider All Forms and Types of Data Throughout Their PLC Work

Given the context of accountability in which educators work today, the goal that we seek as we work together in our PLCs is improved teaching with an eye on student learning. By working together, PLC members can discover ways to improve student learning and help one another improve teaching practices along the way. This vision is maintained by making student data a regular artifact that is reviewed and discussed at PLC meetings. Data include, but are not limited to, student work, standardized test data, formative assessment, summative assessment, authentic assessment, performance-based assessment, and attitude/surveys. By using multiple forms of data to drive your conversations and decisions, we keep the focus of our conversations on our students and their learning.

The types of data teachers bring to the PLC and examine as a part of their work is important. As noted by Taylor (2002), teachers not only need to bring data but they need to bring all data—the good, the bad, and the ugly. A part of your PLC culture must be the willingness to take risks and share the "ugly" data as well as the more successful examples of student learning. It is important to share your own ugly data to demonstrate your vulnerabilities as well as your interest in growing professionally by gaining insight from your colleagues. For when all types of data are shared, PLC conversations will focus on student learning and teacher learning will occur.

Essential Element #9: Healthy PLCs Understand Change and Acknowledge the Discomfort It May Bring to Some PLC Members

Always be aware that change will cause some PLC members, and maybe you, a great deal of discomfort. Change is full of uncertainty. According to Fullan and Miles (1995), "Change is a process of coming to grips with new personal meaning, and so it is a learning process" (p. 408).

One activity that might help you explore feelings about change is engaging in a book study using the book *Who Moved My Cheese?* by Spencer Johnson (1998). *Who Moved My Cheese?* is a metaphorical story of four characters who live in a "maze" and look for "cheese" to nourish them and make them happy. Two of the characters are mice named Sniff and Scurry, and two are "little people" the size of mice who look and act a lot like people. Their names are Hem and Haw. The reactions of these characters vary from quick adjustment to change to waiting for the situation to change by itself to suit their needs. This story is about adjusting attitudes toward change in life—especially at work. Change occurs whether a person is ready or not, but the author affirms that it can be

positive. The overarching principles illustrated in the book are to antici-
pate change, let go of the old, and act as if you were not afraid. These
principles also serve as great principles to guide the work of a PLC.

Essential Element #10: Healthy PLCs
Work With Their Building Administrators

According to DuFour (1999), principals have been called upon to
(1) celebrate the success of their schools and to perpetuate discontent with
the status quo; (2) convey urgency regarding the need for school improvement and to demonstrate the patience that sustains improvement efforts
over the long haul; (3) encourage individual autonomy and insist on adher-
ence to the school's mission, vision, values, and goals; and (4) build wide-
spread support for change and to push forward with improvement despite
resisters as well as approach improvement incrementally and to promote
the aggressive, comprehensive shake-up necessary to escape the bonds of
traditional school cultures. For these reasons, principal support is critical to
PLC work, and PLC work is critical to the effective principal leadership.

As you engage in your PLC, you must recognize the importance of the
school administrator and plan for his or her involvement. He or she can
provide the organizational and structural supports for this collaborative
work to take place. By working closely with the principal and other district
administrators, organizational incentives can support and integrate PLC
work into existing structures. Some districts have been able to integrate
PLC participation into the teacher's professional development plan, and
other districts have allowed teachers to use the PLC work toward the
teacher's recertification credits. Structural and organizational supports
provided by the principal can be critical to the success of a PLC.

WRAPPING THINGS UP

Just like a doctor working with a health care team to ascertain the best
course of action in the treatment of a patient, your work as a teacher
collaborating with colleagues within a PLC is to ascertain the best possible
teaching practices to help all children learn. For this to happen, your PLC
must be a *healthy* place for all members to question, investigate, learn,
grow, and improve practice together. To create a healthy PLC, use the
benchmarks of PLC work discussed in the previous chapters (getting
started, determining a direction for your PLC, creating a PLC action
learning plan, analyzing data, and sharing your PLC work with others) in
concert with the ten essential elements of PLC work shared in this chapter
to guide the work you do as a member of any PLC. In doing so, you create
and operate PLCs that successfully facilitate learning with other educators
who are equally invested in student learning.

Working to create healthy PLCs is more important today than ever. According to DuFour (2004):

> The professional learning community model has now reached a critical juncture, one well known to those who have witnessed the fate of other well-intentioned school reform efforts. In this all-too-familiar cycle, initial enthusiasm gives way to confusion about the fundamental concepts driving the initiative, followed by inevitable implementation problems, the conclusion that the reform has failed to bring about the desired results, abandonment of the reform, and the launch of a new search for the next promising initiative. Another reform movement has come and gone, reinforcing the conventional education wisdom that promises, "This too shall pass." (p. 6)

We hope this book has helped you develop the commitment and persistence to stay the PLC course and work through any initial confusion about fundamental PLC concepts and initial implementation problems your school may have or will encounter as you try out PLC work for the first time. For there is no other element in schools that has more impact on student learning than the personal and professional growth of the adults who teach them. A proclamation made by acclaimed educator Roland Barth (1981) over thirty years ago remains true today: "When teachers examine, question, reflect on their ideas and develop new practices that lead toward their ideals, students are alive. When teachers stop growing, so do their students" (p. 145).

PLC work can keep you alive and growing. It is worth the effort—for the students!

References

Barth, R. S. (1981). The principal as staff developer. *Journal of Education, 163*(2), 144–162.

Barth, R. S. (1990). *Improving schools from within: Teachers, parents, and principals can make the difference.* San Francisco, CA: Jossey-Bass.

Barth, R. S. (2006). Improving relationships within the schoolhouse. *Educational Leadership, 63*(6), 8–13.

Bryk, A., & Schneider, B. (2002). *Trust in schools: A core resource for improvement.* New York, NY: Russell Sage Foundation.

Buffman, A., & Hinman, C. (2006). Professional learning communities: Reigniting passion and purpose. *Leadership, 35*(5), 16–19.

Calkins, L., Ehrenworth, M., & Lehman, C. (2012). *Pathways to the common core: Accelerating achievement.* Portsmouth, NH: Heinemann.

Chard, D. J., Ketterlin-Geller, L. R., Baker, S. K., Doabler, C., & Apichatabutra, C. (2009). Repeated reading intervention for students with learning disabilities: Status of the evidence. *Exceptional Children, 75*, 263–281.

Cushman, K. (1999). The cycle of inquiry and action: Essential learning communities. *Horace, 15*(4).

Darling-Hammond, L. (1997). *The right to learn: A blueprint for creating schools that work.* San Francisco, CA: Jossey-Bass.

Desimone, L. M. (2009). Improving impact studies of teachers' professional development: Toward better conceptualizations and measures. *Educational Researcher, 38*(3), 181–199.

DuFour, R. (1999). Challenging role: Playing the part of principal stretches one's talent. *Journal of Staff Development, 20*(4), 62–63.

DuFour, R. (2004). What is a "professional learning community"? *Educational Leadership, 61*(8), 6–11.

DuFour, R., & DuFour, B. (2007). What might be: Open the door to a better future. *Journal of Staff Development, 28*(3), 27–28.

Elmore, R. (2007). *Bridging the gap between standards and achievement.* Washington, DC: The Albert Shanker Institute.

Erb, T. O. (1997). Meeting the needs of young adolescents on interdisciplinary teams: The growing research base. *Childhood Education, 73*, 309–311.

Friend, M., & Cook, L. (2000). *Interactions: Collaboration skills for school professionals* (3rd ed.). New York, NY: Longman.

Fullan, M. G. (1999). *Change forces: The sequel.* Philadelphia, PA: Falmer.

Fullan, M. G. (2007). Change the terms for teacher learning. *Journal of Staff Development, 28*(3), 35–36.

Fullan, M. G., & Miles, M. B. (1995). Getting reform right. In A. C. Ornstein & L. S. Behar (Eds.), *Contemporary issues in curriculum* (pp. 403–414). Boston, MA: Allyn & Bacon.

Garmston, R. J. (2007). Results-oriented agendas transform meetings into valuable collaborative events. *Journal of Staff Development Council, 28*(2), 55–56.

Gay, G. (2000). *Culturally responsive teaching: Theory, research, & practice.* New York, NY: Teachers College Press.

Goldhammer, R. (1969). *Clinical supervision: Special methods for the supervision of teachers.* New York, NY: Holt, Rinehart and Winston.

Harmon, J. M., Wood, K. D., Hedrick, W. B., Vintinner, J., & Willeford, T. (2009). Interactive word walls: More than just reading the writing on the walls. *Journal of Adolescence & Adult Literacy, 52*, 398-408. doi: 100.1598/JAAL.52.5.4

Hord, S. M. (1997). *Professional learning communities: Communities of continuous inquiry and improvement.* Austin, TX: Southwest Educational Development Laboratory.

Hord, S. M. (2007). Learn in community with others. *Journal of Staff Development, 28*(3), 39–40.

Hunter, D., Bailey, A., & Taylor, B. (1995). *The zen of groups: A handbook for people meeting with a purpose.* Tucson, AZ: Fisher Books.

Jacobs, J. (2007). *Coaching for equity: The transformation of field supervisors' pedagogy in a professional learning community* (Unpublished doctoral dissertation). University of Florida, Gainesville.

Johnson, S. (1998). *Who moved my cheese?* New York, NY: G. P. Putnam's Sons.

Killion, J., & Roy, P. (2009). *Becoming a learning school.* Oxford, OH: National Staff Development Council/Learning Forward.

Kruse, S., Louis, K. S., & Bryk, A. (1994). *Building professional community in schools: Issues in restructuring,* Center on Organization and Restructuring of Schools, Wisconsin Center for Education Research, University of Wisconsin–Madison.

Lambert, L., Collay, M., Dietz, M. E., Kent, K., & Richert, A. E. (1996). *Who will save our schools? Teachers as constructivist leaders.* Thousand Oaks, CA: Corwin.

Learning Forward. (2011). *Standards for professional learning.* Oxford, OH: Author.

Learning Forward. (2015). *Standards assessment inventory.* Retrieved from http://learningforward.org/consulting/sai.

Levine, T. H., & Marcus, A. S. (2007). Closing the achievement gap through teacher collaboration: Facilitating multiple trajectories of teacher learning. *Journal of Advanced Academics, 19*(1), 116–138.

Lieberman, A., & Miller, L. (1992). *Teachers—Their world and their work: Implications for school improvement.* New York, NY: Teachers College Press.

Little, J. W. (1981). *School success and staff development in urban desegregated schools: A summary of recently completed research.* Boulder, CO: Center for Action Research.

McDonald, J. P., Mohr, N., Dichter, A., & McDonald, E. C. (2003). *The power of protocols: An educator's guide to better practice.* New York: Teachers College Press.

Natkin, J., & Jurs, S. (2005). *The effect of a professional learning team on middle school reading achievement: An impact assessment.* Greensboro, NC: SERVE.

Nolan, J. F., & Huber. T. (1989). Nurturing the reflective practitioner through instructional supervision: A review of the literature. *Journal of Curriculum and Supervision, 4*(2), 126–145.

O'Connor, K. (2007). The last frontier: Tackling the grading dilemma. In D. Reeves (Ed.), *Ahead of the curve.* Bloomington, IN: Solution Tree.

O'Connor, K. (2010). *A repair kit for grading: 15 fixes for broken grades, 2nd Ed.* Boston, MA: Pearson Education, Inc.

Reeves, D. (2007). From the bell curve to the mountain: A new vision for assessment, achievement, and equity. *Ahead of the curve.* Bloomington, IN: Solution Tree.

Ronfeldt, M., Farmer, S., McQueen, K., & Grissom, J. (2015). Teacher collaboration in instructional teams and student success. *American Educational Research Journal, 52*(3), 475–514.

Schlechty, P. C. (2007). Move staff development into the digital world. *Journal of Staff Development, 28*(3), 41–42.

Senge, P. (2007). *Society for organizational learning.* Retrieved from http://www.solonline.org/pra/tool/skills.html.

Sergiovanni, T. (1994). *Building community in schools.* San Francisco, CA: Jossey-Bass.

Showers, B., & Joyce, B. (1995). *Student achievement through staff development: Fundamentals of school renewal.* White Plains, NY: Longman.

Southwest Regional Educational Laboratory. (2007). *Reviewing the evidence on how teacher professional development affects student achievement.* REL 2007-22. National Center for Education Evaluation and Regional Assistance, U.S. Department of Education.

Taylor, R. (2002, December). Shaping the culture of learning communities. *Principal Leadership, 3*(4), 42–45.

Tomlinson, C. A. (2001). *How to differentiate instruction in mixed-ability classrooms.* Alexandria, VA: ASCD.

Trimble, S. B., & Peterson, G. W. (2000). *Multiple team structures and student learning in a high risk middle school.* Paper presented at the annual meeting of the American Educational Research Association, New Orleans, LA.

Vescio, V., Ross, D., & Adams, A. (2008). A review of research on the impact of professional learning communities on teaching practice and student learning. *Teaching and Teacher Education, 24,* 80–91.

Wheelan, S. A., & Kesselring, J. (2005). Link between faculty group development and elementary student performance of standardized tests. *Journal of Educational Research, 98*(6), 323–330.

Wheelan, S. A., & Tilin, F. (1999). The relationship between faculty group development and school productivity. *Small Group Research, 30*(1), 59–81.

Yendol-Hoppey, D., & Dana, N. F. (2010). *Powerful professional development: Building expertise within the four walls of your school.* Thousand Oaks, CA: Corwin.

Other Books by Nancy Fichtman Dana and Diane Yendol-Hoppey

Dana, N. F., & Yendol-Hoppey, D. (2014). *The reflective educator's guide to classroom research: Learning to teach and teaching to learn through practitioner inquiry* **(3rd ed.). Thousand Oaks, CA: Corwin.**

This book complements professional learning community (PLC) work by providing an in-depth introduction to another form of job-embedded professional development—teacher inquiry or action research. The book takes both prospective and practicing teachers step by step through the inquiry process including developing a wondering, collaborating with others, collecting data, considering the ethical dimensions of one's research, analyzing data, writing up one's work, assessing the quality of inquiry, and sharing one's work with others.

Dana, N. F. (2013). *Digging deeper into action research: A teacher inquirer's field guide.* **Thousand Oaks, CA: Corwin.**

This book takes off where *The Reflective Educator's Guide to Classroom Research* leaves the reader, providing teacher–inquirers tips for each part of the inquiry process as they are in the midst of doing it (i.e., developing a wondering, developing an inquiry plan, analyzing data, and presenting one's work). A perfect complement to *The Reflective Educator's Guide to Classroom Research*, this book can also be used as a short, succinct, stand-alone text to guide teachers through the inquiry process in a very targeted and specific way.

Dana, N. F., Burns, J. B., & Wolkenhauer, R. (2013). *Inquiring into the common core*. Thousand Oaks, CA: Corwin.

This book tells the story of Woodson Elementary School and the ways the teachers and administrators in this building used job-embedded professional development (the process of inquiry) to better understand their implementation of the Common Core State Standards. In addition, teachers engaged their students in inquiry to actualize the Common Core State Standards in classroom practice.

Dana, N. F., Thomas, C., & Boynton, S. (2011). *Inquiry: A districtwide approach to staff and student learning*. Thousand Oaks, CA: Corwin.

This book describes the ways engagement in PLC work and inquiry fit together for all constituencies within a district—principals, teachers, students, and coaches. This systems' overview of PLCs and inquiry and the ways the processes can connect improved practice to student achievement enables the reader to enhance learning for adults and students across an entire district.

Yendol-Hoppey, D., & Dana, N. F. (2010). *Powerful professional development: Building expertise within the four walls of your school*. Thousand Oaks, CA: Corwin.

This book provides a bird's-eye view of numerous job-embedded professional development strategies. In addition to a chapter on PLCs, chapters focus on book studies, webinars and podcasts, co-teaching, conversation tools, lesson study, culturally responsive and content-focused coaching, and inquiry.

Dana, N. F. (2009). *Leading with passion and knowledge: The principal as action researcher*. Thousand Oaks, CA: Corwin.

This book applies the notion of job-embedded professional development to administrators as it takes principals and assistant principals through the process of action research step by step.

Dana, N. F., & Yendol-Hoppey, D. (2008). *The reflective educator's guide to professional development: Coaching inquiry-oriented learning communities*. Thousand Oaks, CA: Corwin.

This book focuses on coaching the inquiry process within PLCs. Much of the material in *The PLC Book* is derived from this text. If you are interested in more details about coaching a PLC however, you will find additional material and coaching tips in this book.

Yendol-Hoppey, D., & Dana, N. F. (2007). *The reflective educator's guide to mentoring: Strengthening practice through knowledge, story, and metaphor.* **Thousand Oaks, CA: Corwin.**

This book explores the mentoring of new teachers from many different angles. The reader is introduced to seven different mentors and their work with mentees, with each mentor demonstrating different components of effective mentoring through the use of metaphor: Mentor as Story Weaver, Mentor as Jigsaw Puzzle Enthusiast, Mentor as Tailor, Mentor as Coach, Mentor as Mirror, Mentor as Interior Designer, and Mentor as Real Estate Agent.

Index

A SAGE Company

Helping educators make the greatest impact

CORWIN HAS ONE MISSION: to enhance education through intentional professional learning.

We build long-term relationships with our authors, educators, clients, and associations who partner with us to develop and continuously improve the best evidence-based practices that establish and support lifelong learning.

Solutions you want. Experts you trust. Results you need.

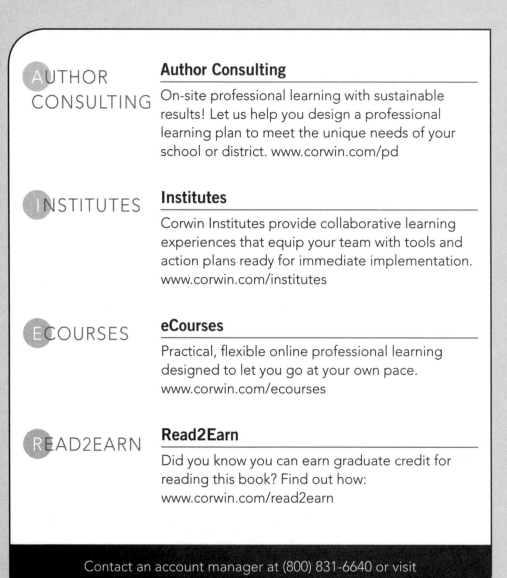

AUTHOR CONSULTING

Author Consulting

On-site professional learning with sustainable results! Let us help you design a professional learning plan to meet the unique needs of your school or district. www.corwin.com/pd

INSTITUTES

Institutes

Corwin Institutes provide collaborative learning experiences that equip your team with tools and action plans ready for immediate implementation. www.corwin.com/institutes

ECOURSES

eCourses

Practical, flexible online professional learning designed to let you go at your own pace. www.corwin.com/ecourses

READ2EARN

Read2Earn

Did you know you can earn graduate credit for reading this book? Find out how: www.corwin.com/read2earn

Contact an account manager at (800) 831-6640 or visit **www.corwin.com** for more information.